moments of *extraordinary* courage

moments of extraordinary courage

by katherine turner

Copyrighted Material

This book is a work of creative nonfiction. It reflects the author's present recollections of experiences over time. Some names and characteristics have been changed, some events compressed or excluded, and some dialogue has been recreated.

Copyright © 2021 by Katherine Turner
www.kturnerwrites.com

All rights reserved. No part of this book may be reproduced or used in any manner without written permission of the copyright owner except for the use of quotations in a book review. For more information, address: kt@kturnerwrites.com.

First edition: April 2021

Editing by Olivia Castetter and Kayli Baker
e-book formatting by Jo Harrison
Cover design by Emily Wittig
Cover photography by Nordwood Themes

Library of Congress Control Number: 2021907147
Library of Congress Cataloging-in-Publication Data available upon request.

ISBN 978-1-7344230-3-7 (ebook)
ISBN 978-1-7344230-4-4 (paperback)
ISBN 978-1-7344230-5-1 (hardcover)

Josha Publishing, LLC
Independent Publisher
www.joshapublishing.com
Haymarket, VA

Printed in the United States of America

for everyone battling silence

may these words inspire you to find
your own courage

contents

mute: a poem v
the silencing 1
a writer who doesn't write..11
loose 19
intolerance and ignorance 25
a word for nonconsensual...39
#metoo 47
lorena bobbit wannabe 55
chameleon suit 61
therapy and a letter..69
in-process...79
work variance 89
picture on the wall 95
eighty bucks 103
rabbit 111
remember when…..125
dominoes..135
acknowledgements...143
further reading..147
about the author 149
by katherine turner 151

Mute

Mute
Press the button

Oh, shit
What did I just say?

I can't tell my story
I've already said too much
If I speak again, they'll call me a liar
"That didn't happen"
"You can't be serious"
"If that was true, we'd have known"

They say
They say
They say

But I lived.

I endured
I survived

I fought a war and no one heard the first shot
But I felt it
The wound that consumed me
The life that it took
The blood that I bled without a stain to prove
That shot that began as a thought
That thought that became an action
Telling me I was his to use
Hers to use
And I'd only ever lose
But I stood up.

I fought back
I lost the battle
Then I won the war
I've got scars they'll never see
These things I carry inside of me
These secrets, this past, my determination
That I will be the last
It ends with my generation!

Now I stand victorious
Not waving a flag
If I hoist my colors
The truth will be uncovered
The truth will be revealed
And I'm not supposed to talk
About the wounds time will never heal

Mute
Press the button

What if this is the moment that starts a movement?
What if this didn't have to be stunned silence
My audience desperate to escape
What if this is just the end of the first act
And I've left them on the edge of their seats?

Mute
Press the button

Pause

Oh, shit
They're waiting for me to speak

What if I let them see?
What if I tell the story?

My story
My story
Not his
Not hers
My story

A story of survival
A story of a battle
A story of the war
And the soldiers
Still waiting for their revival

If I break my silence
Will chains be broken with my eloquence?

Unmute

-Olivia Castetter

the silencing

I recently stumbled across a quote that read, "Sometimes you don't actually know how traumatic something you went through is until you talk about it like it's just some random anecdote, and then you realize the table's gone silent, and your friends are all staring at you like 'what the fuck?'" When I first read those lines, I laughed—I couldn't help it, really. I understood just how much truth resided within those words.

When we're children, we tend to find whatever happens to us, whatever we see happening around us, to be normal. How could we not? It's the only thing we know. No matter how awful or traumatic the experience may be, it's just "how things are." As we get older, sometimes we become aware that what we went through wasn't normal; sometimes we don't. And even when we're aware those experiences weren't the norm for most, the truth remains that those experiences were normal—*are* normal—for us.

Humans are social creatures—even those of us who are introverts need social interaction. We crave being part of a group, a community of some kind and the acceptance that brings, the certainty that we aren't alone. When we've survived a trauma, that drive for acceptance can be amplified as a result of what we've experienced. I remember growing up and begging the universe to make me "normal," dreaming about fitting in with my peers; I knew I wasn't like them, though pinpointing exactly why when I was a child was a bit more difficult. As I got older, I began to better understand what things were accepted as normal and what things weren't, and I worked to hide those that threatened my ability to be accepted.

Even so, there were situations when I attempted to chime in, to contribute to a conversation, and encountered blank stares instead of the guffawing laughter I was anticipating. Facial expressions indicative of shock. Disbelief. Pity. Disgust. I've even encountered anger for speaking about certain things from my childhood, being called a "downer" for my participation in a conversation, even though I was only sharing what had happened to me. The events in my childhood, no matter how upsetting they may be for others to hear, are simply a part of who I am. And sometimes there is no way for me to contribute on a topic with an anecdote that will make the other participants smile or feel warm and happy.

This type of experience is intimately familiar for survivors. When we attempt to embrace our vulnerability, to take a chance on opening up and honestly sharing our experiences, we are treated—however unintentionally—as if what has happened to us is our fault. As if we have a responsibility to protect others from any discomfort they may experience as a result of learning what we've survived. As if we have committed an indiscretion by virtue of having been at the receiving end of some sort of trauma. It becomes abundantly clear in our minds that there is something wrong with us and we feel more isolated than we did before we attempted to speak up.

And while this is damaging enough, it's what happens next—after the shock of our companions—that I think we don't talk about enough as a society. That I believe we *need* to talk about if we're ever going to see meaningful change. Most of us who have committed the faux pas of telling the truth will laugh uncomfortably, likely brush it off and shrug, assure whoever's there that it's really not *that* big of a deal, and in the same breath ask about another's recent promotion or trip to a concert or new significant other. Or maybe we make light of it, belittling our own pain, even as our hearts are racing. Make fun of the thwacking sound of our father's belt buckle as it landed on our young and tender skin and made it bleed. Or denigrate ourselves with laughter over the fact that we were so aware of the moonlight coming through a small opening in the structure that trapped us, reflecting off the teeth of our rapist as our body was violated.

In her book, *Know My Name,* Chanel Miller tells the reader about the night she revealed to her parents that she was the victim in the Brock Turner assault case. She's just referred to some of the details of the case in the news, minimized what happened to her—"It was just his fingers, so that's good"—and then stood there smiling.

How many of us survivors are now groaning inwardly because we recognize exactly what she's describing? How many of us can recall situations from our past when we did the same thing, smiling about something that's destroying every fiber of our being, just to keep from upsetting someone or making someone uncomfortable? And while most people have a natural instinct to protect those they love from harm, from pain of any sort, society has also taught us that our pain is shameful, something to be embarrassed about. That when our pain stems from something that makes others uncomfortable, we should keep it to ourselves. That the discomfort someone may experience as a result of learning what happened to us is more important than the pain of having lived through and survived that experience. In this way, we have been conditioned to believe that we must "fix" our mistake when we say something that another finds unsettling.

And so we smile, we laugh, we shrug. We change the subject, redirect, suddenly have an appointment we're late for and rush to exit. Anything, really, as long as it shifts the focus from us and the "crime" we've just committed by shocking our companions. We want to fade back into the background where we were before we tried to step into the light, back into the background where our soul has been hiding since those unspeakable things happened to us.

I call this The Silencing. It began with those traumatic experiences and persisted over the years at the insistence of a society that values superficial comfort over truth and openness. But the truth is that we will never find a society that supports survivors and values healing over ignorance—we will never cultivate a culture of compassion and understanding—until we recognize that our own hands are sometimes the strongest of those trapping us in a cycle of The Silencing. And the only way to prevail is to face our fears and act, knowing the outcome is uncertain.

That doesn't mean we go to battle against the world. It doesn't mean we allow anger to direct our actions, or become reckless with other people's lives or emotions, or suddenly become suspicious and distrustful of others and their intentions. It also doesn't mean we don't feel weak and vulnerable and afraid at times, or need to step back and simply remember how to breathe. And it doesn't mean we need to be strong every second of every day.

But it *does* mean that we stand like a stone pillar in our truth when the forces of doubt and discomfort attempt to topple us. It means we demonstrate the compassion we seek to find in others as we endeavor to open their eyes and ears and hearts. It means we persist against the tempest of how things have been by planting our feet and persisting along the path to change. And it means that in moments of intense vulnerability and apprehension, we find the courage to refuse to be displaced from our authenticity.

To live in this way—to gift integrity and loyalty to *ourselves* through these moments of extraordinary courage—does get easier over time. It becomes more natural and comfortable, less threatening and intimidating. Like much in life that's new to us, the beginning is by far the most difficult, and often seems an impossibility. Fear whispers into our ears that we will fail, that we will drive away our loved ones, our friends, that our souls will feel emptier than before if we allow ourselves to be vulnerable with the ones we love most. But fear lies to us. The reality is that honoring ourselves by bringing all of us into the light will bring us a love that no one can take away from us without our permission, a love that can sustain us no matter what is happening around us or who is or isn't in our lives. This love is self-love.

On the following pages, you'll have an opportunity to step briefly into my shoes—hear my thoughts and feel the intensity of my emotions—during some of the most arduous and fearsome moments of fighting The Silencing in my life (you can read more detail about the traumatic events responsible for The Silencing in my memoir, *resilient*, and on my website). Some of these experiences are loud and combative while others are quiet and subtle, and yet, they all have something in common. Each represents a moment—a single moment—when I had to make a choice between the comfort and familiarity of the known found in The

Silencing, and the fear and ambiguity of un-silencing myself and speaking my truth.

My hope for you as you turn these pages is that you will immerse yourself in my life-defining moments of daring to battle The Silencing, get lost in the complexity of emotions and thought-patterns so characteristic of facing our deepest fears, and then, somewhere along the way, find yourself—the You that perhaps no one has ever seen. I hope that you will smile in recognition and hold out your hand, ready to move forward as one. That you will intertwine fingers with your soul, take a deep cleansing breath, and then step into your own moments of extraordinary courage.

"The definition of vulnerability is uncertainty, risk, and emotional exposure. But vulnerability is not weakness; it's our most accurate measure of courage."

-Brené Brown

a writer who doesn't write

Aside from a handful of poems—and by handful, I mean maybe five—I stopped writing for pleasure after I took a creative writing class my junior year in high school. Even for that class, I wrote only poetry and micro-fiction. I hadn't recreationally written something that was longer than a page since I'd shared a novella with my teacher in fifth grade.

I'd spent winter break feverishly writing a story that had been in my head, one my teacher had encouraged me to put on paper. I'd written short stories before, but this was different. It was longer and had more action to the story—really, it was a short novel.

My main character was Cassie, a teenage girl whose father had sexually abused her almost nightly for years before he'd walked out on her and her mother. Cassie's mother had no idea about the abuse and had become a severe alcoholic after Cassie's father left. The story follows her sudden and unexpected friendship and then romantic relationship with a classmate named Mark, who protects her from ill-meaning teenage boys and teaches Cassie that she's not at fault for having been abused, that she has a right to say no, and that she should never do something she's not comfortable with; he taught her how to set boundaries about her body.

After editing the story until I thought I could do no more to improve it, I shared it with my beloved teacher. She read and returned my manuscript to me, but she didn't know how to talk to me about her discomfort and worry instigated by reading a story about sexual abuse that was written by a ten-year-old. Instead, her eyes filled with tears and she was unable to find words, saying nothing to me about the story.

A few years prior, I'd been sexually abused by my cousin, and then by a family friend. I knew I hadn't liked it and I'd had nightmares about it. I knew I'd done the unthinkable—molesting a teddy bear in front of a room full of strangers in a courthouse—in order to prevent it from happening to another little girl. And yet, at the same time, I didn't understand how abnormal my experiences were for a child my age. As a result, I mistook the reaction I saw in my teacher for her trying to find a nice way to tell me my story was terrible and I shouldn't try to write anymore. My interpretation was only reinforced when I later overheard her talking to my foster mom about my story and she called it "not normal."

I threw out my story when I got home and vowed never to write another one, never to share anything important that I'd written with anyone ever again. In retrospect, this is likely why I started to write so many letters; I wrote letters to my parents, with whom I had no contact, and letters to my brothers, whom I saw infrequently at the time. I wrote letters to my friends and—as I got older—my boyfriends. I even wrote letters to myself, and I journaled until my foster mom read one of my letters and my journal once; then I hid any letters I wrote and stopped writing in my journal entirely. I couldn't keep myself from writing poetry, though, despite my efforts—I had a deep need to somehow express myself using the written word. Part of the reason I took a creative writing course during my junior year was so I'd have an "excuse" to be writing. But even in that class, when I had opportunities to choose assignments that would result in prose longer than a page, I opted for something with a shorter form.

Twenty-three years after my teacher handed my novella back to me, I typed the first word of my first book—*Finding Annie*. I'd been fighting against a soul-deep desire to write for decades and found myself unable to continue turning my back on an activity that is as much a part of who I am as the trauma I've survived. But even once I'd made the decision to lay down arms and cease battle against my true passion, I didn't fully commit to myself. That experience with my teacher when I was ten still burned strong in my memory even though I understood as an adult what was behind her reaction. *People don't want to read the kinds of stories I want to write*, I thought.

But I *had* to write.

My heart yearned to write about love, a topic that has garnered my interest and fascination my entire life; giving love, receiving love, pining for love, platonic love, romantic love—all of it. At the same time, I also couldn't stomach the idea of writing a story about a woman who wages a war against a history of trauma, coming out on top after many bloody battles, and then having it classified as contemporary romance. After much internal debate, I decided I would have to give up on the love aspect because the message of healing was more important to me.

Looking back and talking about my thoughts before I typed that first word makes me smile and shake my head a bit. I realize how naïve I was for thinking I had any choice in the matter. As soon as I started typing, my heart and my soul took over and I had very little say about the story that unfolded. A story of love and loss, a story of pain and healing, a story of regret and redemption and forgiveness. The characters are different, the story details have changed, but the *premise*—the role of love to help us heal and find our boundaries and self-worth after abuse and trauma—is exactly the same as what I wrote when I was ten.

When I finished my first draft barely eight months later, I had six books written and the key points and scenes for a seventh, the final book in my Life Imperfect series. The lives of the main characters are messy—*really* messy—and filled with mistakes and pain. But they're also full of love and forgiveness and healing. The characters are gloriously imperfect because life after trauma is like that. Nonetheless, imperfect doesn't mean any less beautiful, and that's something I wanted to show. I wanted people to read about the parts that trauma survivors keep to themselves, that we hide out of fear and shame. I wanted to tell the story about the unhappy, messy, and spectacularly raw and beautiful middle between surviving and thriving. And when I read through my own words, I felt I had done just that.

My feeling of pride, however, only lasted until I remembered that a key part of showing those parts to people was putting my story out there for them to read—I'd be putting my words into other people's hands. Suddenly, all I could hear was my teacher saying my writing wasn't normal, and I knew my story was unlike anything else out there—unlike anything *I'd* ever read, anyway. My soul, though, was telling me the same thing it did when I wrote that story about Cassie all those years ago—that if I was writing the stories I wanted to read, that there are in fact others who want to read them, too. Normal or not.

I joined some writers' groups on Facebook for exchanging manuscript drafts, but I still couldn't put myself out there. Instead, I offered to do swaps for others and said my manuscript wasn't ready yet. I read manuscript after manuscript but continued to drag my feet about sharing mine. One of my friends read my draft, as well as the unedited drafts of the rest of the series, and provided feedback that was kind and encouraging, but I convinced myself she was only trying to be nice, trying not to hurt my feelings. She dispelled that notion with honesty and genuine evaluation; she told me the parts that made her laugh, the parts that made her cry, the parts that made her furiously angry, and the parts that made her heart ache, and I decided it was time for me to step out and send my story to strangers.

With the emails typed to my beta readers, my draft attached, all I needed to do was click "send," but the voice of doubt was loud, the words "not normal" blasting into my ears as if by megaphone. My hands shook and I had to reach down and wipe my palms over my pants to get the sweat off. Pain seized my chest with the onset of an episode of premature heartbeats, a heart condition triggered by heightened and sustained anxiety, and my stomach churned. My lips tipped up on one side. *I'm having a panic attack, right now. And I only know what is happening to me—finally—because of this book,* I thought. These sensations, the resulting inability to think or process words—incoming or outgoing—or tolerate noise, or in any way function without either being left utterly alone or drinking alcohol to excess, was something I'd struggled with my whole life. I'd always thought it was just me—just another way I wasn't normal like other people, one of my many personal "oddities." I'd spent considerable effort learning how to mask it when it happened, to hide it from view so others wouldn't know.

A few months before, in addition to the friend who read the drafts of the entire series, there was another woman who read an early draft of the first five chapters of *Finding Annie*; she was the first person to lay eyes on any portion of my manuscript. I likely never would have sent it to her, but she was my husband's coworker and he'd told her I would send it to her without asking me first. Near the end of her email, she wrote, "I think you have done a good job of making the reader feel the panic attacks that Annie is feeling."

Everything around me had faded into the background as I stared at those words, reading them over and over and over. Panic attacks? I'd written Annie in many ways to be like me; I gave her parts of my trauma history. I gave her a story with sexual assault at the heart of it, and I gave her some of my "oddities" because I'd been desperate for a story with a heroine who sounded like me, who seemed to struggle the way I did. But I'd had no idea there was a name for what she experienced—what I experienced—that it wasn't just a craziness about me that I needed to keep hidden from the world. I fired up my search engine and spent hours researching panic attacks. Each source of information seemed to be describing me; I felt like I was looking into a mirror. It was the first moment I realized maybe I wasn't as weird and crazy as I'd always thought. Maybe I didn't need to keep parts of myself hidden. Maybe I wasn't the only one who struggled in that way.

As my fingers hovered and trembled violently over the enter key on my keyboard, the only thing standing between me and having my manuscript in beta readers' hands, I thought back to that discovery courtesy of the woman who'd read my first five chapters, thought back on how much had already changed in the previous few months since that had happened. Maybe if I hit send, my story would be rejected. Laughed at. Returned unread because it was just too weird or sad or realistic.

But *maybe* someone else would recognize themselves the way I'd recognized myself. Maybe it would prompt self-discovery that could lead to healing for someone else. *Maybe* the simple act of putting myself out there as I really am for once would prompt my own journey of self-discovery and healing. I was terrified, but I also wanted to stop keeping parts of myself in the dark, in the silence.

There was no way to tell what would happen next, but it was a risk I needed to take—for myself, for others. My eyes filled with tears, one slipping free as I closed them. I inhaled sharply, and then pressed my finger down on the enter key.

Sent.

loose

I spent the summer of 2000 living in South America with a Chilean family for a summer exchange program, returning to the US shortly after my sixteenth birthday. Before departing for my trip abroad, I had broken up with my boyfriend of the last two years—friend for even longer—after he'd become violent with me. During that breakup, I discovered that he'd slept with more people than I could count on two hands while we were dating and paid people to lie to me about his newfound drug and alcohol habit. The breakup itself, what I learned about his deceit, and the end of our friendship sent me into an emotional tailspin—I was hopeful my time away would help me to find myself.

While in Chile, I went with one of my host sisters and another exchange student to a discotheque for a night of entertainment Chilean-youth-style. At the time, I smoked cigarettes and decided at some point during the night of dancing and sipping on Piscolas that I was going to step outside for a smoke. One of many Chilean teenage guys who'd danced and chatted with us since we'd arrived decided to accompany me for a cigarette. We walked outside a few feet from the doors, but I was only a couple drags in when I started shaking with cold—it was winter in Chile and I was not appropriately dressed to be standing outside in the middle of the night. He noticed that I was shivering and offered for us to sit in his truck to finish our smokes. I quickly agreed.

We finished our cigarettes mostly in silence, and I decided to take a moment to rub my icy hands in front of the vent blowing warmish air before we headed back into the building. After a moment, he raised the windows, then said in broken English that he wanted to kiss me. It sounded romantic to me, and I was still reeling from my recent breakup, so I agreed. Kissing wasn't all he had in mind, however, and he wasn't going to take "no" for an answer.

I attempted to push him away, but wasn't able to stop him from trying to get past my clothes. Luckily, he froze when his hand came into contact with the menstrual pad I was wearing; I was on my period and only wore tampons if I had no other choice. *Un*luckily, he wasn't going to just let me leave until he got what he was after and chose my mouth for the task.

When he was satisfied and let me out of his truck, the passenger door opening only from the outside, I told no one. I smiled at my host sister and assured her it only took so long because we were talking, that I was fine.

loose

That night, I listened to my host sister and another exchange student breathing as I lay awake, terrified someone would figure out what happened—or, as I saw it back then, what I'd been stupid enough to allow to happen. The other exchange student I spent the next day with kept looking at me with questions in her eyes, but I ignored them. When I went back to my host family's home later at the end of that day, I plastered a fake grin on my face and assured them I'd had a blast at the discotheque. I resolved to eradicate the assault from my memory and pretend it had never happened.

Not long after I returned stateside, my ex called me and said he wanted to catch up, that he'd missed me over the summer. Despite the reservations I had, the feeling in my gut that told me to refuse, I agreed. I was desperate for something resembling normalcy, for feeling loved in some way, and I'd really missed him, too; he'd been a significant part of my life for years. He picked me up and drove me to a secluded orchard behind his parents' house. He asked me about the landscape and I traveled back over the summer in my mind, telling him every detail about the country and culture I'd fallen in love with, carefully avoiding any mention of the guy at the discotheque. He smiled as he listened and I got lost in the stories I told him until I suddenly realized that he was no longer sitting next to me on the hood of his car, but was in front of me and running his hands up the exposed skin of my thighs below my shorts.

I had never told him no to sex—even when I'd wanted to, I'd never felt I had a right to deny him—but

I couldn't stomach the idea of sexual contact of any sort right then. I stammered out that I'd thought we could just talk, but he only responded that he'd missed me and continued what he was doing. His face kept morphing into that of the guy from Chile, and I felt nauseous and screamed in my mind for him to stop, but he didn't. I was barely aware of what he was doing until he paused suddenly.

"You're loose," he said, his voice loud and hard. "Who'd you fuck in Chile?"

Tears stung my eyes, and I clenched my jaw, ready to risk his temper, ready to fly in the face of my undercurrent of fear of him becoming violent toward me and shove him away from me, screaming at him to go fuck himself, when shame washed over me, dragging my shoulders down instead. How I could be so indignant when I was stupid enough to almost get myself raped? So idiotic that I'd been forced to give a stranger a blow job?

I told him that there had been no one since him; he told me he didn't believe me. He began moving again, but with a violence that hurt me, and then said, "You feel that? You feel how loose you are? I know you're lying. I know you've been having sex with someone else."

Could a tampon make me seem loose? I wondered. I had used one earlier in the summer during my first period on the trip—could that be why I was loose to him? I wanted to suggest that, wanted to keep arguing, to tell him he was wrong, tell him what had actually happened the one time it had been a close call, but I couldn't. He already didn't believe me; he'd never believe what had actually transpired. And even if he did, he would blame me for what happened.

After that, I thought I'd finally be able to forget what had happened that night in South America and got back to work on erasing my memory. But it came back again a few months later. I'd started dating a previous boyfriend again—the first serious boyfriend I'd ever had, and with whom I'd shared a deep connection from the day I'd met him—and we were on a walk together when it happened. He said that my ex told him I'd had sex while I was on my trip abroad.

My lungs expelled all air from them and didn't want to cooperate to draw in more. I couldn't believe what I'd heard and asked if my ex had really said that. My boyfriend assured me he had, that my ex had said that he slept with me when I got back and that I was loose.

Loose.

Hearing that word again sent a tidal wave of rage through my veins and I went on the offensive, told him that my ex was telling the truth—that we'd had sex and that he'd called me loose. Then he asked if it was true that I'd been with someone over the summer, insisting he wanted to know.

"It doesn't matter what I say—no one ever fucking believes me anyway," I bit out.

"I believe you if you say it's the truth," he replied. "Period."

I stared at him for a moment as my eyes flooded with unexpected tears; my chest felt like it was caving in on itself and my rage was suddenly gone. I wasn't sure if he really would believe me or not, though he was the only person in my life who had a tendency to believe me when it mattered most. Turning, my eyes gazed into the distance at the soft, rolling mountains surrounding my hometown. In my life's experiences to that point, it had always been worse to speak a painful truth and not be believed than it was to just keep it to myself, to not take a chance on becoming vulnerable and having that vulnerability trampled or used against me. But in that moment, in the seconds before I next spoke, I realized how much weight that secret was burdening me with and decided that, this time, I'd rather risk rejection, risk being disbelieved, than keep it hidden.

"I didn't sleep with anyone while I was gone," I said quietly. "I don't know why he thinks I'm loose, but it's not from having sex, because I didn't." I inhaled deeply, my jaw trembling. "I was almost raped," I added, my voice cracking as my tears spilled over.

Before he even voiced that he believed me, my body already felt weak with relief from having broken my silence and spoken the words aloud.

intolerance and ignorance

By the time I entered foster care when I was eight-and-a-half years old, I was familiar with various types of prejudice. The one I had the most extensive experience with was related to poverty; my family was poor. Not lower-middle-class-wishing-for-that-cool-new-toy poor, but well-below-the-poverty-line, clothes-and-shoes-with-holes, hungry-and-begging-on-the-streets-for-money poor. Immediately before my younger sister and I were removed by social services, we lived in a trailer park and were bullied by the other children for being the poorest family there. For always being hungry. For always being dirty and smelly.

When we begged for money in the local shopping center, many people skirted wide circles around us as if we were diseased and contagious. Others would literally walk into us as if we didn't exist at all. When my sister and I snuck into the local Subway, hoping a paying customer would leave their scraps of uneaten food on the table when they left, we were often chased out like criminals rather than being seen as the two hungry children we were. Some customers even looked at us as they threw a half-eaten sub in the garbage before leaving, making a point of ensuring we knew they thought the trash bin was more worthy of their uneaten food than my sister and I were.

We were also scorned because our mom was in a relationship with a woman—the same woman for whom she'd left our dad. Adults and children alike sniggered in front of us and called them names like "dyke" and "pussy-eater." My mom and her girlfriend had a friend in the trailer park—a trans woman—who they called names like "fag" and derided our family for having a friend *like that*.

While we were living in our fifteen-foot trailer that already housed four with no electricity or running water, we took in a young man who was homeless; my mom's girlfriend had found him wandering the streets alone. He was mentally disabled, and while he was in his early twenties, his mental state was more akin to a ten-year-old and his family had thrown him out for it, as if he'd had a choice. We didn't have much—nothing, really, save a roof over our heads at night—but we shared what we had with another human being who had been discarded because of a genetic disability.

And though I didn't realize it at the time, I'd already encountered racial prejudice, having been born to a mixed-race couple, introducing the only white person and only mixed children into my dad's extensive family. It was only recently that I started making connections between their behavior toward my siblings and me, their baseless distrust of me and extra abuse when my father and I lived with them, the rarity of my mother's presence at the frequent family gatherings, and the one thing that made us so different from everyone else—our skin color.

The prejudice I encountered didn't end once I entered foster care, either. During my first week in my new school, a boy singled me out in the hallway between the lunchroom and our classroom and pointed at me as he shouted, "Nigger!"

If skin could burst suddenly into flame, mine would have. My body would have been consumed by fiery fingers borne of shame and embarrassment. I froze, wishing I could disappear into nothingness, feeling guiltier than ever that I even existed as the word rolled around in my mind. I wanted to be invisible, out from under the eyes of the other kids who were all staring at me as if they were waiting for me to assure them it wasn't true. I hadn't thought we looked that different before that moment, but I was suddenly hyper-aware that we actually did; my skin was noticeably more brown than theirs. I realized I was a mixed-race kid living in a very white rural town in the South, and it felt like I'd just learned that it was a crime to look like I did. The teacher made him say that he was sorry, and I nodded my head, but all I heard was that shout reverberating in my mind.

It wasn't long after that incident that I had to complete a standardized test form. Embarrassed to have a question before we even started the test, I raised my hand and waited for my teacher to reach me.

"How do I fill in race/ethnicity?" I asked.

"You fill in the bubble next to 'white,'" she said with her brow furrowed.

"But I'm not," I whispered. "I'm biracial—I'm black *and* white."

"Oh," she said, her head drawing back in surprise; she'd obviously never thought about the dilemma I was now facing. "Well... you can fill in black if you want, or you can fill in white. Just pick one."

As my teacher moved on, walking between rows of desks, I stared down at the demographic question on my paper. *Pick one*, she'd said. But how did I do that? I was too white to be black and too black to be white. I didn't fit in to any category I was allowed to choose. How did I pick just half of who I was? And which half? My mom's half or my dad's? The seconds ticked by loudly on the clock on the wall as my pencil hovered over first one, then the other bubble. With each breath, I felt more alone, less like I belonged than ever before, and a mixture of shame over being something no one accepted and anger that it even mattered took root in my chest.

I learned quickly that it wasn't a good idea to volunteer my heritage to folks in the area, not sure what kind of a reaction I would encounter. It was pretty much guaranteed to be negative if there was a rebel battle flag (what you likely picture when you think of the Confederate flag) on their porch or attached to their truck bed or stuck to a car window. But the absence of the flag wasn't any kind of guarantee of acceptance, either. I had a friend whose parents wouldn't let me go to their house again when I told them, and another *intolerance and ignorance*

whose father beat her after finding out she and I were hanging out with one of the few black kids in town. When I met a boyfriend's parents for the first time when I was fourteen, he told me right before we walked in that I shouldn't tell them I was biracial; according to him, they weren't racist, they just didn't want him dating a person of color.

On the other hand, one of the black kids I was friends with turned out to be making fun of me behind my back for "trying to be black." Then there were the kids in the group home I lived in as a young teen who called me names and stole my belongings for being mixed.

Often, I just smiled and nodded if someone guessed that I was Latina or Mediterranean instead of correcting them (unless they were then calling me a "spic" because they didn't like anyone of Hispanic origin either). Sometimes, though, I was sick of trying to pretend I was someone I wasn't because of being afraid of how people would respond; I was simultaneously ashamed of being mixed and furious that I felt that way. On those occasions, I rebelliously shouted it as the first thing I said when I met someone as a sort of test to see how they'd react, then regretted my behavior for weeks or months afterwards.

People who seemed to be genuinely nice would snicker and point and make fun of the kids in our school who were physically or mentally disabled, loudly making jokes and calling them names like "retard" loud enough for them to hear and sometimes even to their faces. I hated them, too, just as I hated the unknown person who kicked out the man we'd welcomed into our trailer before I went into foster care. I wanted to scream at everyone that they were just people, that being disabled in some way didn't mean they weren't human, and it didn't mean they couldn't hear you, and it certainly didn't mean they didn't have feelings. I knew my advocacy for the other judged and ridiculed students was yet another way I wasn't like my peers, another thing that made me different and not normal, but I simply couldn't keep quiet about what I was witnessing.

I glared at the kids making those comments and walked over to say hello and talk to the kids they were making fun of. *Fuck them*, I'd think. I felt the need to protect anyone who was wronged in whatever way I could. Even if that meant I was only having a conversation when I passed them in the hall and ensuring they wouldn't hear the comments around me. I'd walk down the hall with them to finish our conversation, and I'd wave whenever I saw them, smiling. And on those occasions where I felt I was still too quiet, where the anger inside was simply too much, I'd lift my hand behind my back as I walked and flip my middle finger toward the kids being unkind.

When a friend of mine came out, I was one of about five people who knew he was gay; it was too dangerous for him to come out publicly in the ultra-conservative area in which we lived. Anyone who even speculated was viciously mean. His own mother threatened to kick him out as a young teenager when she suspected,

intolerance and ignorance

telling him she'd rather him be dead than gay, and her sentiment was by no means unusual.

One year in high school English, we had to choose a controversial topic for a research paper, I—and about half of the class—chose gay marriage. However, I was the only one who wrote in support of the sensitive topic. I was afraid of what might happen—I was well aware I was nearly alone in my sentiments in my county—but the weight of responsibility I felt to stick up for those being discriminated against exceeded my fear. My teacher, a woman I respected and who was there for me in ways I desperately needed when things started falling apart at home, marked my paper down a letter grade because of my take on the topic, her feedback in red pen commenting on how immoral it was to be gay, how it was a choice despite what my sources said, how disgusting even the thought was. Next to a picture I'd attached with two women facing each other in their wedding dresses and holding hands, she'd written, "YUCK!!!!!!"

I hated her in that moment—hated every person who had ever said something bad about my mom or her girlfriend, every person who said something offensive and hurtful about or to my friend, felt burning hot rage in my chest with every tear I saw him cry. *Why couldn't people just be fucking people?* I kept thinking.

The only place I felt safe in that regard was at home; my foster mom was not like most folks in the area. She saw people as people and not as the color of their skin or sexual orientation or anything else. If my friend had been kicked out like he nearly was, she assured him we had a warm bed and open arms for him. And we would have for anyone else who needed it, too. But outside those walls, I had to make a choice every day whether I would smile and nod and bite my tongue, succumbing to the pressure to keep my thoughts and truth to myself, or whether I would risk ridicule and rejection to speak out.

We attended church every week like the other families in our town; my foster mom had my sister and me baptized as Episcopalians. But sometimes, when we traveled about forty miles south to a large indoor farmer's market, we'd also swing by a Quaker meeting house nearby. We attended a Unitarian Universalist church for a while when I was a teen, and every few years my foster mom attended a weekend Buddhist retreat at the Bhāvanā Society. She had books on all different kinds of religions—a topic she'd studied in college and found fascinating. But when my sister and I told our friends, it wasn't very well received— especially by their parents. Some friends' parents hesitated to let us hang out, afraid our religious curiosity might wear off on their children or simply because even considering a different religion meant we were heathens or devil worshippers. We lived in an area that was ultra-religious—mostly Baptist—and religious tolerance was a foreign concept.

It seemed that everywhere I turned was one prejudice or another, people treating me or others like they were less than human for any number of reasons; you couldn't just be accepted for who you were. The list I already had of things about myself that I needed to hide, to keep to myself, to make sure people never found out, only continued to grow.

Aside from moments when my anger and frustration burst forth in an explosion of defiance, I internalized all the prejudice I experienced, all the intolerance I saw around me. Years passed in this manner, and then, during the height of the Black Lives Matter movement, I read a piece on outrage culture by writer Jacob Nordby about what happened on Twitter when he posted a snippet of an interview with Morgan Freeman after he was asked how we stop racism. Mr. Freeman had responded, "Stop talking about it. I'm going to stop calling you a white man, and I'm going to ask you to stop calling me a black man."

Responses to his tweet went crazy, people outraged and condemning Mr. Freeman's words. He was speaking strictly of race relations, but the underlying concept was the same—people are people. The same concept I'd thought about with frustration most of my life, wondering why we couldn't just stop focusing on things that didn't really matter, differences that had nothing to do with who we were as human beings.

I shared the post and my reaction with a writer friend, noting that I wished I was brave enough to speak out, and she encouraged me to do so anyway. Her encouragement was the last bit of motivation I needed—I wrote my piece *Mixed in America: A Perspective on Discrimination*, drawing on my myriad experiences with it over the course of my life, my unique perspective on what was happening, and what I believe we need to do before we'll ever see lasting improvement, regardless of what kind of discrimination it is. Of course, there were several drafts, with much editing between, before I decided to share with a handful of friends and family so I could incorporate additional feedback to improve the universality of the piece before publishing it. I expected a mix of praise and constructive criticism from everyone, but there were a few responses for which I'd been unprepared.

The first reaction I received back was one that surprised me. My closest friend, who moved to the United States when she was a child and became a citizen when she was a young adult, shared that she became very emotional reading my piece, identifying strongly with not fitting in, having been rejected by American kids as well as kids from her native France. The next few reactions were a mix, much like I'd initially anticipated, and then there were the last two responses.

One came from a friend. I'd known when she didn't respond at all that there was something she was hesitating to say. I wanted to understand the what and the why, so I reached out to her and asked for her thoughts. What it boiled down to was that she didn't believe I had a right to have an opinion on racism and discrimination. I look like a well-adjusted white woman (with a tan), and through dialogue with her, it became apparent that even though she knew bits and pieces of my childhood, it was how things appeared on the surface that drove her reaction. That she was reading my piece and responding as if I *was* a well-

intolerance and ignorance

adjusted white woman without a care in the world, rather than a woman still battling a childhood filled with abuse, trauma, and discrimination. That even though she read snippets in the piece, she forgot that I had first-hand experience of the types of things I was talking about and had a right to contribute to the discussion of those matters.

The other came from a member of my foster family; she said she thought I was missing the point of the current movement to address racism, that I reminded her of Rodney King tearfully asking, "Can't we all just get along?" When I read her thoughts—that she maybe never intended for me to read directly, since they were forwarded to me by another family member—I felt like I'd fallen on my back so hard I had the wind knocked out of me. I couldn't breathe or tear my eyes from reading and re-reading her words.

Between the last two responses, I was devastated on a very personal level. My experiences were—not for the first time in my life—being dismissed. I questioned why I thought I had something of value to say. I've always been aware that I think about things differently from most people and battled both a love and hate of that fact, though I'd more recently fallen into the former category, recognizing that it wasn't isolated or coincidental that whenever I go out of my comfort zone about things I feel passionate about, things that deal with basic precepts of humanity, people respond strongly. People share that I found a way to explain or demonstrate or paint a picture of the topic that allowed them to see it from a perspective they'd never previously considered. But this experience left me excusing away all those memories, convinced that I'd deluded myself that I had a unique and valuable message, and I decided I was too scared of the reactions I might face if I followed through. For days, I re-read my piece over and over as my finger hovered over the button to delete the post before it was scheduled to be live.

Then, I thought about what my friend who initially didn't respond had said after our back-and-forth on the topic—that she realized that, because of my experience, I had a right to an opinion and that *she* did not as a white, cis-gendered woman.

I had appreciated her gesture when she apologized and said this to me, but I didn't fully agree, either; part of the point I was trying to make was that we shouldn't be silencing anyone, for any reason. I thought again with fresh eyes about what my family member had said and realized that I wasn't misreading anything or making an impotent plea, as she'd intimated. I was making the same point that Morgan Freeman did during his interview, and facing my own version of the backlash he received. And then I remembered that part of the problem we face, part of the reason it's proliferating so many years into differing movements to eradicate various types of prejudice and discrimination, is because *different* is frowned upon—it doesn't matter where that difference originates.

In this case, *different* was my perspective. And the automatic self-doubt and dismissal I felt when encountering that discrimination against my

intolerance and ignorance

worthiness to contribute my ideas is how people on the receiving end of prejudice remain there, having been conditioned to believe deep down that the discrimination is deserved simply because someone else thinks so.

I felt nauseous and couldn't sleep for days as I edited and rewrote parts of my essay in an effort to avoid more people reacting like my friend and my family member. I cried because I was so afraid of what would happen, had nightmares about losing the people important in my life, but decided that being true to myself, saying what needed to be said for those who are too beat down to say it themselves, was worth the risk. And then I published that essay that bore my truth, my heart, my soul, as a gift to myself on my thirty-sixth birthday.

a word for nonconsensual

Whenever I talk about my first memory of being sexually abused by my teenage cousin, I say I was seven because that's easier. Really, it was a few weeks shy of my seventh birthday. My biological father and I were living temporarily in his sister's house when it happened and the adults weren't far away, but they were all drinking heavily and we'd been warned about having our backsides beaten raw if we disturbed them. After my cousin was done pinning me down and touching me despite my protests, just before he let me go, he warned me not to tell anyone. He threatened to hurt me if I did, and also assured me he'd deny it and that everyone would believe him over me.

I was afraid, but decided I was going to tell my dad anyway; he was my *dad*. In spite of the abuse and neglect, I loved him, and I felt certain he loved me back. More importantly, I was positive he would protect me. Instead, though, he got angry—at *me*. He yelled at me and called me a liar and made me promise him that I'd never tell another soul what I'd told him. I cried and agreed before I got spanked.

Just over a year after that day, I was molested again; this time by a friend of my biological mother's while I was living with her not many months before I entered foster care. This man wasn't a teenager like my cousin; he was old enough to be my grandfather. Again, alcohol was involved, though instead of behind a closed door in the next room, my mom was only feet away, passed out after excessive consumption. I called out for her; she never heard me.

As the man insisted that I close the few feet of distance between us, I battled internally over what to do with my mom so close yet unconscious. I didn't want to obey the man, but felt I had no choice and ultimately did as he instructed. By the time my mom's girlfriend arrived afterward, the man was passed out as well and I was the only one awake in his trailer. She knew immediately that something was wrong, but I was afraid to tell her. I thought back to what happened with my cousin, how my dad had called me a liar and been so angry and sworn me to silence and secrecy. I thought about how easily angered my mom was and desperately didn't want to get in trouble and get spanked if I said something.

Nonetheless, I told her what had happened and then shared what my cousin had done to me as well. I felt guilty for having broken my vow of silence to my dad, felt guilty for making my mom and her girlfriend so upset. And later, I battled regret over saying anything at all when I was sitting in a courthouse

a word for nonconsensual

having to relive what my mom's friend did to me so they could prosecute him. I blamed myself even then for everything that happened to me; I felt it was a punishment for not having been a good enough child, and I felt it was my fault for not having been able to stop it. But the fact that my mom and her girlfriend had believed me stuck with me.

It was that memory of being believed that overshadowed my father's disbelief almost exactly five years later when I was thirteen and made the decision to tell my close friend and my boyfriend that his two brothers—one of whom was my close friend's boyfriend—had trapped me in an enclosed area and forced me to have sex. I wasn't sure how to describe it—the only concept I had of rape at the time involved violent physical struggles that left the victim in a bloody and tattered state. I knew what his brothers had done wasn't consensual, that I had said no and had begged to be left alone, and that my words had been met with threats. That there had been no way I could have physically escaped. That my body had frozen when the oldest brother touched me.

Despite my faith in them, my friend and boyfriend didn't believe me; without that physically violent struggle to get away, they refused to consider what I told them about the encounter lacking consent, being against my will. Instead, I was told if I hadn't wanted it to happen, I would have physically fought to get away. My trust in people—including myself—was shattered that day; anything that remained after my early childhood was now gone. I was sure that, despite my fear, my frozen state—despite my subsequent nightmares and emotional pain that contributed to my habits of self-harm—I must have subconsciously wanted it to happen. So I told no one else what happened. I looked down in shame and said nothing when I heard people whisper about me having cheated on my boyfriend and "fucked" those brothers, and I did my best to bury and forget as much of what happened both the night the brothers trapped me as well as the night I lost my friend and boyfriend.

Nearly twenty-one years later, a few months shy of my thirty-fourth birthday, I was at a brewery local to my hometown, visiting with my foster mom who still lived where she'd raised me. It was a beautiful summer's day, the sky a rare blue for the time of year, sun shining hot and bright except when a fluffy white cloud floated by. We'd just sat down with an ice-cold beer as my two little girls chased butterflies in the field of tall grass and wildflowers adjacent to where we relaxed in the shade.

"Do you remember Rudy?" my foster mom asked.

I was instantly catapulted twenty-one years back in time, my ex-boyfriend's face flashing before my eyes. Rudy had been his adult mentor; my ex was fourteen when I'd met him and his brothers, while I'd been twelve. My stomach clenched instinctively as his older brother's face was next to come up from the shadows, the iciness of his eyes and the terror he'd instilled in me from the very first time he greeted me by biting my neck until it bled.

a word for nonconsensual

I remembered the way his teeth had glinted in the moonlight that spilled through the open top of the teepee *that night* a few months after I'd met them. The sound of the laughter coming from my boyfriend's younger brother as he readied himself to go first. I remembered the fear that paralyzed me as the older brother's threats hung in the dense, humid air along with the smoke from his cigarette, and I realized I couldn't escape the small enclosure and the two boys. I remembered the sensation of my tears tracking down my temples and the rocks and earth under my back and shoulders as my body jerked back and forth unwillingly in the dirt.

I remembered the longing I had for my boyfriend to wake from his alcohol-induced slumber, inside and on the other end of their house, and my intense regret that I had snuck over to see him that night. I remembered the relief I found in the pain caused by scrubbing my thighs raw to bleeding once I'd made it home that night, and the following week of depending on that relief to keep suicidal thoughts at bay until I decided to take a chance and tell someone.

I remembered when I told my boyfriend and my best friend how they accused me of lying, just as my father had years before when I'd been molested by my cousin. I remembered swearing that it wasn't consensual, that I hadn't wanted it to happen, and how the pain—and later bruises—where my best friend's blows landed as she assaulted me couldn't compare to the hurt in my heart. And I remembered how I'd spent years believing that I'd somehow been at fault and wishing that I'd died when she pushed me down a flight of stairs the night I told her.

I remembered all these things in the span of a few breaths after my foster mom asked her question. I felt a sinking in my gut and the skin on my face tightened uncomfortably as the edges of my vision blackened. I began sweating profusely until it was running in little rivulets from my armpits toward my wrists and my chest felt too small for my heart to move. My eyes darted around where we sat, scanning the other people near us over and over and over, as if a person could appear out of thin air.

What if those brothers had never left the area? What if they were there and I just hadn't seen them yet?

I was adept at hiding my discomfort and my panic; if my foster mom didn't notice my eyes darting around—and she wouldn't, because she's always drawn to watching the behavior of other people around us when we're in public—she would never know. I carried on with the conversation, even though I felt like I would suffocate if I didn't get into my car and drive until I ran out of gas.

"He said you always had all the boys spun up over you," she said. "Instigating trouble between the brothers. He wished you would just leave that family alone."

I froze as time came to a standstill. My heart didn't beat; my lungs didn't expand with air. Suddenly, I felt like I was spinning out of control and my vision narrowed to a pinpoint. Normally, I would look down and try to redirect the conversation to a more diverting topic, but I was sick of keeping it all in; when I opened my mouth, something entirely different rolled off my lips.

"He wished *I* would leave *them* alone?" I bit out. "*I* got *them* spun up?"

My voice was fading, and I tried to swallow to alleviate the sudden dryness that was at fault, but I couldn't because my tongue was in the way, having suddenly become too large and thick for my mouth. I looked to my right, out at the wildflowers growing in the field against a backdrop of the mountains surrounding my hometown as the bright day seemed to darken and fade into grey before me, trying to breathe against the tightness in my chest and ignore the burning in my eyes. My jaw trembled slightly, and I gritted my teeth to steady it.

And then it happened.

"His brothers raped me," I whispered.

If the earth had opened up at that moment and swallowed me into its bowels never to return to my life, I would have been grateful. *Relieved*. The depth of exhaustion that took over after my confession was incomprehensible. The gut-wrenching fear of her reaction almost kept the words inside my mouth— would she disbelieve me as my father had about my cousin? As my ex and my former best friend about my ex's brothers?

But I was too tired to stop the words from coming out. Tired of keeping secrets, tired of hiding parts of myself. Tired of pretending things that had happened... hadn't. Each thing I hid, each secret I kept, each event I pretended hadn't occurred carried with it an unimaginable weight—I simply couldn't stand and continue any longer if I didn't start shedding some of it.

My foster mom turned from her people-watching to study me and I was intensely uncomfortable under her scrutiny, the waiting and the unknowing suffocating me. Finally, she spoke.

"I'm so sorry," she said quietly. "I... I had no idea."

I don't remember much from the rest of that day aside from my dizzying relief that she believed me, everything cloaked in a dark haze as if I'd been blackout-drunk, though I'd only had a single beer.

But I'll never forget what came before that black hole in my memory, never forget everything leading up to me using the "r" word almost twenty-one years after it had happened when I'd just turned thirteen, finally breaking the deafening silence about what really happened that night.

#MeToo

Around the same time I made the decision to delve into my past and confront my childhood trauma and abuse, I noticed many of my friends and acquaintances on social media posting stories followed by #MeToo. One by one, I read them—several times—and felt pieces of my heart breaking off and falling away; it was shattering for these abused and assaulted women, and it was also shedding layers of protection I'd spent a lifetime carefully building up. With each piece that fell, I cried both for the women I was reading about as well as for myself.

I remember reading about people who were skeptical about all the #MeToo stories, even some people I knew were less than enthusiastic, from thinking women were making things up for attention to settling personal vendettas to trying to get rich. There were others I knew—primarily in older generations—who didn't indicate one way or the other whether they believed these women but simply felt it was airing one's dirty laundry, sharing something you should want to keep a secret. Whenever I listened to these people, I became angry. Sometimes I argued, but often I was paralyzed by anger and fear of confrontation, and I wasn't sure how to persuade them to be more open-minded without telling my own secrets. And then I'd get back online and look for more stories.

To a bystander, it may have seemed a bit morbid that I couldn't seem to read enough of these women's stories. But I derived no enjoyment from knowing others had experienced similar abuses. Rather, I found comfort that I wasn't alone and was inspired by the strength and bravery I knew it must have taken for them to share what happened to them. I admired them for defying fear and shame and societal pressure to speak their truth.

But every post, every article, every essay I read left me with a deeper and deeper sense of guilt; I'd read these women's stories, but I hadn't yet shared any of my own. I felt like a hypocrite, like I was betraying these women by rooting them on from the shadows, safe in the familiarity of what I'd been doing for decades: hiding. Until one night, I could no longer bear the growing shame and guilt born of my silence, born of the suffocating layers of years of denial and suppression, and decided it was time to tell my story—at least part of it. And if I did that, I could never go back to lying to myself, pretending again that I was fine and those things hadn't happened to me.

I typed the words into one of my personal social media accounts and refused to allow myself to re-read them—I *knew* if I did, I'd end up deleting the entire post. I'd revealed so very little with what I'd written, but I was utterly terrified of what would happen once the post was visible. My fingers shook violently as they hovered over my keyboard and I could feel my resolve, my burst of courage, beginning to fade. Gritting my teeth, I clicked the "post" button, and then rushed to the bathroom where I threw up.

> "Since I started seeing the hashtags in my newsfeed with increasing frequency, I have had an urge to share but felt ashamed and been afraid of what those who don't know might think about me at the same time I feel such admiration and support for those who have been sharing their stories. I realize that I am so tired of feeling afraid, ashamed, disgusted with myself, like I'm partially to blame.
>
> #metoo
>
> From being molested twice before I was eight years old to having my boyfriend's brother threaten me if I didn't have sex with him when I was 13 to having a friend's father tell me to take my shirt off and show everyone my boobs, and more. I refuse to feel shame any longer."

-October 2017

I'd done it! I felt an enormous amount of regret initially, but after a few long days and sleepless nights, I was proud of myself. I felt brave and like some of the weight I'd carried for so long that I thought it was just another part of me had faded away.

After that experience, I continued to seek out and read as much as I could of people telling their stories of trauma and abuse, sexual and otherwise. Each story gave me a little more courage and determination to part with the shame that felt so much a part of who I was. In a way that perhaps only other survivors will understand, seeing myself in others' stories brought a unique solace.

But I also began to feel a new type of shame—the kind that comes from being dishonest.

I felt I may as well have lied in my post by way of omission; I'd barely scratched the surface of what happened to me, and I felt that my inability to divulge any more meant I was both a fraud and a failure, that rather than brave, I was really a coward.

That shame was still there a few months later when I made the decision to start writing again and dove into drafting my first series. Over the next year, I developed the story of Annie, Rob, and Lucas (the main characters in *Finding Annie* and my Life Imperfect series), who work to heal, find love, and overcome traumatic childhoods. Along the way, I put a lot of thought into how I wanted to structure my author website, what kinds of topics I would address, even what I would divulge about myself, and ended up engaged in an internal tug of war.

I grew up in a world that operated based on compartmentalizing, strictly separating personal from everything else; it was unprofessional and unacceptable to do otherwise. And it was something that already came naturally to me from my childhood—no matter what abuse or neglect was occurring, no matter how painful the gnaw of hunger, no matter how many nightmares kept me awake all night, I excelled in school. I could carry on a conversation with just about anyone with a perfect mask intact because the personal had been placed into its box, closed up tight, and set aside. As the years passed, that kind of behavior was encouraged. Praised, even.

This left me conflicted when it was time to make decisions about my website. I certainly didn't want to muddy the waters between professional and personal, but the reality was the personal was the driving influence behind the professional for me—they really couldn't be separated—not then, and not now. But marrying the two not only went against the grain of everything I'd learned, but it was also intimidating because I was so new to sharing those personal aspects I'd kept so carefully hidden for so long; I knew there was a risk I'd chicken out at some point and hide the personal again if I didn't do something to ensure I could never sever that connection. So I decided to write an intimately personal post on a topic I was passionate about, though new to discussing so publicly.

moments of *extraordinary* courage

I wrote a post about consent, using my own early teenage rape as the example to demonstrate what I was trying to convey. The words poured out of me in a flood, and I edited furiously until I felt I had a piece I could be proud of. A piece I'd be wowed by if someone else had written it. A piece that would make me feel compassion rather than judgment. I loaded the content to my website, formatted to my liking, and scheduled the publish date for the next Friday, which was a few days away.

My blogging process involves completing my editing in a Word document, only uploading the content and scheduling the posting date once everything has been finalized. As a result, I don't often return to my scheduled posts before they go live. But this one? I returned to it dozens of times over the next few days, reading and re-reading and re-reading my words, making an occasional tweak. But instead of feeling a growing confidence that the piece was ready, I became plagued by more and more doubt.

What was I thinking writing a post so personal? A post that told so much about the past I'd kept hidden for so long? Would I lose the supporters I'd gained? How would my family feel about me being so open about what happened to me? Would my daughters grow up one day and be embarrassed or ashamed of what I'd written? What if the people involved in the event discovered that I'd shared it publicly?

In my mind, my entire reputation as not only an author, but as a person—a friend, a wife, a mother, a daughter, a sister, an employee—was at risk because of my decision to bare part of my past. I was in danger of losing face with everyone in my life and opening myself up to retaliation. Was that really something I wanted to risk?

The day before the post went live, I opened up the draft and read through it several times. My stomach was roiling and my heart was racing painfully in my chest as I took rapid, shallow breaths. I decided I couldn't do it; it was too much, a step too far from my comfort zone, too far from what everyone I knew thought they knew about me, everything they expected from me. I was just too scared to go through with it. I clicked to delete the post and a box popped up on the screen telling me I'd just selected to delete my post and asking me if I was sure. I moved my cursor over the "continue" button to complete the deletion, but then I hesitated.

Was I sure? Really sure? Did I *really* want to go back to the stifling silence I'd been fighting so hard to escape? This was my opportunity—did I really want to give it up? I thought about all those women who'd inspired me with their #MeToo stories, how much I'd healed because of their courage. I thought about where I'd be emotionally if they hadn't been courageous enough to speak and wondered how many women I might be able to inspire, to heal, if I could dig a little deeper and find a little more courage. I'd thought my comfort and sense of security were more important than speaking out, but was I sure? I stared at that dialog box as my hand shook, at the words "Are you sure?" and realized, *No, I'm not sure, damn it!*

I clicked on "cancel," closed my browser, and shut down my computer, my mind racing to come up with something to keep me occupied until the next morning when the post would be live. Come hell or high water, I was *not* returning to silence and the way things had always been.

lorena bobbit wannabe

I was molested twice in my early childhood. My teenage cousin molested me when I was seven, and when I told my father, he didn't believe me. When my mother's older friend molested me about a year later, she believed me, and the police report that followed led to the involvement of social services, which ultimately led to my placement in foster care when I was eight-and-a-half.

A few years into foster care, when I was eleven, my crush asked me to be his girlfriend and go to the movies with him, but only under the condition that I would perform oral sex on him in the movie theater—no oral sex meant no date and no girlfriend status. I refused, but was left feeling upset and confused.

My first real boyfriend was intensely sexually focused—a product of his abusive home—and I had sex for the first time with him when I was twelve, not long before he slept with someone else while we were dating.

Then, when I was barely thirteen, I was raped by my next boyfriend's two brothers, and only months later, an older high school guy I didn't know grabbed my ass when he walked past me in track practice. Two years later, our school brought in a sexual predator for the girls' varsity soccer coach—a man who ogled and commented on our bodies and badgered us for dates—and we weren't believed when we complained to the administrators.

After I was raped, the guy I dated placed a fairly high value on the presence of sex in our relationship, and I discovered when we broke up that it wasn't confined just our relationship—he'd had sex with thirteen other girls during the two years he and I dated. The summer we broke up, I narrowly escaped being raped by a guy in a foreign country; instead, I was forced to perform oral sex on him before he let me go. When I got back to the US, my ex used my feelings for him to pressure me into sex, then accused me of being loose and didn't believe I hadn't slept around. Only weeks later, he invited me see his band perform and then dedicated the song he'd written for me the year before to another girl—the last one he'd cheated on me with—which was an entirely different kind of betrayal and emotional blow.

I ended up back with my very first boyfriend, who continued to cheat on me, culminating in him sleeping with my best friend's little sister, which marked a rage-filled end to our relationship around my seventeenth birthday, though not before I met his grandfather and was subjected to him talking about my "nice and sizeable rack."

lorena bobbit wannabe

Reeling from everything that had happened, I decided to drink until I forgot one night shortly after the breakup in the company of people I thought were my friends... Two of them took advantage of my intoxication and inability to consent, adding two more to the tally of males who'd sexually assaulted me.

The morning after that party, I could no longer fully internalize my pain, my anger. I thought back over my history, over all the events I've listed here, replayed them in my mind, felt my heart constricting, my skin covering with filth. Felt the surge of self-hatred and self-disgust, the breathtaking guilt and shame. I struggled to breathe through the intensity of the feelings of unfairness that any of it had happened, that I'd kept nearly all of it to myself, too afraid of what would happen to me if I told someone because of what happened the few times I did. As the roiling emotions settled, two rose to the surface, overtaking all the others.

Rage and hatred.

Something snapped deep inside and it was suddenly like there was a veil in front of me. I couldn't look at or even think about *anyone* of the opposite sex without an outpouring of those toxic emotions. I'd kept them inside for so long that I no longer could—and they came bursting out of me violently. I viscerally hated all males. Men and boys alike, strangers or even those I'd known who had never been anything but kind toward me. I hated them equally. If I saw a male, my face contorted in disgust and ire; if he looked at me, I flipped him off. If I even thought their eyes *might* have ventured even an inch from my face when they looked at me, I released a string of obscene vitriol bordering on verbal abuse that would have had me grounded for months if my foster mom heard. If they tried to talk to me, I told them to go fuck themselves. I hated them. All of them.

And I wanted to hurt them.

It seemed to me the whole problem—everything that had happened to me—came down to the penis between a man's legs. In my mind, that made the solution pretty simple: get rid of the offending anatomical member. Without the source of the problem, the problem would simply go away.

I started dreaming at night and daydreaming during the day about ripping the penis off every male I knew, even every male I saw. I spaced out during class at school, drawing pictures of myself holding the bloody appendages in my hands and the newly de-penised men crying. I swore if any male ever tried to stick their penis in my mouth again, I'd bite down and rip it off with my teeth.

It was only a few years before that every news station in the country was covering the trial for Lorena Bobbit. She was in a violent and sexually abusive marriage, and one night she cut off her husband's penis after he raped her. She'd been demonized by much of the press but I was awed by her actions. I idolized her for doing something about what was being done to her in a way that ensured it would never happen again—at least not from *that* man.

lorena bobbit wannabe

I fantasized about meeting a castrated male and falling in love. I envisioned having conversations during which he looked into my eyes, being valued for my company and my intelligence, for my physical strength and my compassion. I imagined always feeling safe and unpressured because he would have no sexual interest in me—the idea was blissful and made me cry with wanting it to come true.

During this phase, I was more explosive, more hostile, more combative, than usual. In a way, I was combating my fear of rejection for speaking the truth by intentionally ensuring the outcome—in that way, it would be what I expected rather than an unknown. If I was hostile, *of course* no one would respond well to me. If I was so verbal and explicit about my thoughts of castration, *of course* I wouldn't attract loving attention. If I was so outwardly violent and aggressive, *of course* I wouldn't be seen as weak or suffering.

My peers nicknamed me Castration Queen. Some found it funny, some encouraged me, and others avoided me; I'd clearly come unhinged to them, and it was safest to keep their distance. I could see the expression on their faces that clearly said, *what's her problem?* and *she's crazy*. Part of me thought, *I am—so leave me the fuck alone!* But part of me was only further angered by their reactions.

To those on the outside, there seemed to be a disconnect between my life and my behavior. To me, though, there was a clear connection, so the confusion my behavior created in others was infuriating and came out as increased aggression. I didn't understand how my anger was so befuddling and I was sick of trying to just ignore my frustration.

I knew when the lid came off those parts of myself I'd banished and all my pent up pain and fear and rage came hurtling outward in the form of castration fantasies that my behavior was risky. I knew that I could possibly permanently alienate anyone who cared about me, everyone *I* cared about. I knew that I may get into trouble for my belligerence and off-the-charts vulgarity. I even knew there was a possibility I'd get stuck in that heightened state of anger for the rest of my life—that once it started, there may be a never-ending stream of it I might become powerless to rein back in.

It was a risk I had to take, however, because the alternative of suffering in silence would have far-reaching consequences as well. I understood in that moment that if I didn't in some way speak up about what I was experiencing emotionally, I wouldn't otherwise be able to cope, that even my self-harm habits of burning and cutting would be insufficient. I was on a narrow ridge and had reached the end; I could no longer take a step forward the way I had been. On either side of me was an abyss and I had to choose between them. On one side was unsilent rage, on the other was silent death.

And while death sounded easier, I chose rage. For the first time in my life, I stepped fully out of the silence and was heard.

chameleon suit

I've heard people who've been through trauma as children described—by others and themselves—as chameleons, particularly social chameleons. Whatever the situation dictates, they become, donning whatever personality seems most appropriate considering the setting and other participants. The concept makes a lot of sense to me. The ability to be whatever those around you expect is a defense mechanism—a deeply rooted one—born out of a survival instinct. At some point, that was the only way to be safe, and over time, that became automatic. Sometimes people don't even realize they're doing it.

I was always aware on some level when I was the one it was happening to. I knew that I felt inauthentic but was often helpless to do anything about it. I'd certainly learned at a very young age that being yourself, that kind of vulnerability, would be punished. It was unwanted. I'd smile and nod even when I was screaming in my head loud enough to drown out the voices around me. Even once I'd managed to find a person here or there that I could speak the truth to on occasion, being in a social setting was different and more emotionally treacherous.

Part of my journey to heal once I decided to turn inward and address my unresolved trauma involved being aware of when I donned my chameleon suit and actively working to shed it—to only present my authentic self—regardless of the particulars of the situation or attendees. I was making a commitment of authenticity to myself. It turns out that decision revealed I have deeply rooted and fairly severe social anxiety, though again that makes sense when considering my childhood and how unsafe I was around others, both physically and psychologically. I knew my anxiety would diminish with time and I would be able to participate like those around me—*without* the assistance of alcoholic beverages—and that in the meantime it was okay if I felt awkward, struggled with how to engage normally, fumbled my way through conversations.

Of course, remembering that it was okay to be uncomfortable, that it was okay to be myself even if that wasn't what people were expecting, was often a challenge all its own. I'd been on the planet for more than three decades when I made the decision to shed that chameleon suit I'd developed in my earliest years.

I felt I was making pretty good progress when my husband, kids, and I attended a party for a friend of the family. We'd been there for a while and I'd just started my second beverage, even though most of the faces were new. My heart was beating irregularly, but I'd not allowed that to drive me to becoming intoxicated, even after several awkward conversations that ended abruptly. Overall, I was proud of myself and my resolve to remain true to myself.

At the time, I was nearing the release date for my debut novel and receiving questions from those who knew about how the process was going, if everything was on track to occur on time. One of those friends—my husband's boss—asked a number of questions related to my new writing career. For the first time that evening, I really loosened up and the conversation flowed naturally; writing was something I could easily chat about as long as the other participant in the conversation desired. And then, inevitably, he asked about other writing projects on the horizon.

After giving some background on some of my other fiction works in process, I turned to non-fiction and mentioned that I was also working on my memoir.

His eyebrows shot up his forehead. "Your memoir?" he asked, incredulous.

I felt my anxiety surge, as if a boiling liquid had been poured into my veins; within a few heartbeats, my body was on edge, I was sweating, my face was tight, and I had an intense urge to disappear into thin air. Even so, I forced myself to respond. "Yup, my memoir. The first, anyway—there may be more than one."

He laughed, heartily, his head moving side-to-side in disbelief. "What are you, like sixty?" he joked.

In an instant, I was no longer a mid-thirties adult, excited that someone was taking an interest in her passion. Instead, I felt like I was crumbling, like an ancient stone wall hit with a battering ram. All my newly-discovered confidence disappeared.

I was seven years old, trying to convince my dad that my cousin had molested me as he accused me of lying, or begging my mom not to make me choose which parent I loved more as she ignored me and insisted I make a choice immediately, or screaming at my dad to come back as he shut out my voice and intentionally walked onto a busy highway.

I was eight years old, pleading with the social worker not to take my sister and me from our mom without us saying goodbye, then being told to stop crying and get over it. I was growing up in foster care to the chorus of "children should be seen and not heard" and being told to quiet down because I was too loud.

I was thirteen and begging my boyfriend and best friend to believe me that my boyfriend's brothers had raped me as they turned their backs on me, calling me a slut and assaulting me.

I was instantly every insecurity I'd ever felt, in every moment of being silenced or told I wasn't qualified to contribute my experiences. I opened my mouth and my jaw flopped around like a fish for a moment with no sound coming out because I'd lost the voice I'd poured my heart, soul, and sanity into finding.

As I struggled to speak, my instinct was to just shut my mouth, excuse myself either to the bathroom to give in to the tears fighting their way to the surface or to go refill my wine glass and drink until I didn't care. To then carefully pull on the chameleon suit I'd abandoned and fasten it tightly so it could never again be removed and leave me exposed the way I was right then.

But then I thought about the other moments in my life that I'd battled the silence, moments in which I thought my body might kill me before the first few seconds after the silence was broken had passed. I thought about the moments after, once my body believed I wasn't in mortal danger and the anxiety settled to a dull roar, the moments in which I felt a kinship and loyalty deep within my soul for having stuck up for myself.

If I turned to flee in that moment, I felt I'd be betraying myself in every moment I'd fought so hard to drag myself out of silence. And then I'd be there again, in that deafening place of inauthenticity. *No,* I thought. *I can't do that—I can't ever go back to that place again.*

"No," I finally replied, looking at a spot on the wall over his shoulder; eye contact was more than I was capable of in that moment. "But I have lived through enough experiences to be."

"*Really?*"

"Yes, really. Maybe more. Experiences no one should have."

"Really?" he said again. "Like what?"

I bristled at his obvious disbelief; I wanted to say, *How dare you not believe me—after everything I've been through in my life, after everything I'm going through right now to get these words out?* I let the spark of anger catch and spread over the span of several seconds, careful not to let it take over, but simply provide enough fuel to keep me from turning back. With a final deep breath, I parted my lips and let it out—no sugar-coating, no softening of language to make him more comfortable.

"Like being sexually abused and not believed. Like watching my biological parents try to commit suicide. Begging on the streets for money and having to hide some of it from my biological mother so she didn't spend it all on alcohol instead of feeding us. This is before I went into foster care when I was eight-and-a-half." I paused and took a breath, determined to get the next line out, struggling as I still do today. "And then being raped by my boyfriend's two brothers when I was thirteen."

His eyes rounded and he drew his head back. "Wow." He shook his head slightly. "I had no idea. Huh."

He looked away and took a slow sip of his drink as everything I said replayed in my mind and self-doubt immediately set in. And then I started to panic. *Oh, shit. Did I really just say all that to my husband's boss? What is he going to think? Fuck, fuck, fuck!*

I opened my mouth to say something—*anything*—to "fix" what I'd just done only to realize there wasn't anything I could do; even my chameleon suit couldn't undo the past. What was done… was done. I couldn't take it back—the words were already said. Besides, there was nothing to "fix," I reminded myself. Despite how my body felt, I hadn't done anything wrong. I was simply slipping back into taking responsibility for things I'd had no control over, assuming the shame for wrongs perpetrated against me, and feeling guilt for the fact that those things made other people uncomfortable to know.

The things I lived through as a young child—the things done to me against my will—are not my fault or my responsibility to carry. I have no obligation to hide or soften the trauma I've experienced simply because it may bother someone else if I call it what it really is. Society had me convinced most of my life that I was simply too much and needed to be quiet, to keep those uncomfortable topics to myself. That if I absolutely had to talk about them, to use other words; words that are gentler, less alarming and upsetting for others.

Words like "difficult childhood" instead of "emotional and sexual abuse and neglect."

Words like "spanking" instead of "physical abuse."

Words like "nonconsensual sex" instead of "rape."

But I realized as I sat in my discomfort that even the choice of words was a type of silencing in itself. That soft language paints a picture that's more palatable for others, but also misleading in that it's not what actually happened. That choosing words with definitive accuracy is as important as choosing to speak at all, and is the only way to do away with that chameleon suit.

therapy and a letter

Throughout my upbringing in foster care, I was occasionally required by Social Services to attend therapy. I don't recall much about my therapists or sessions from my early childhood, although I *do* remember the therapist I saw as a late teen. His name was Joseph.

He was soft-spoken and kind and patient. When I first started seeing him, I'd sit and stare at the wall in tense silence for the entire session, my body poised for flight in case he tried to do something untoward. My body was sure being in a room alone with him for an hour—the door shut—meant extreme danger. As the weeks passed, though, I began to relax and even look forward to my time there.

I'd arrive and make a cup of hot tea and chat about whatever was going on in school or soccer. Occasionally I talked about my sister or a fight I'd had with my foster mom. Often, I shared my plans for college, which I was in a constant state of analyzing and tweaking. But no matter what questions he asked or how kindly they were delivered, I refused to talk about my early childhood, my boyfriends (past or present), or any of the myriad assaults I'd survived.

Despite my lack of willingness to talk about anything of real substance related to my struggles, he never became frustrated with me; he never pushed me to the point of resenting him. And he was incredibly perceptive. He noticed tiny changes in my speech patterns or breathing rate and would ask me if I was okay when I got lost in whatever thoughts were the catalyst of the changes he noticed. I always lied and said the same thing, "Yeah, why?" to which he'd respond by explaining the changes he'd noted.

I'd think about what he'd noticed—changes that had escaped me—and connect them with my thoughts. Sometimes I unraveled what that meant; other times it was too painful and I pushed it aside and tried to just forget about it. Then I'd look up and see him watching me, his face always open and inviting, but without that unmistakable expectation in his eyes. And when he was worried, there was an extra crease in his forehead.

I knew he was a father himself, and often thought to myself that he was probably a really good dad. I tried to imagine him being my father, how he would have reacted to the news that my cousin had molested me. I was sure he would have believed me, unlike my actual dad. I felt a comfort and trust with Joseph that I'd never had with any other man, but even that wasn't enough to get me to turn inward; I was too scared of what would happen if I spoke those things aloud.

therapy and a letter

Regardless, my relationship during the year or so that Joseph was my therapist solidified my belief in therapy as an effective tool for psychological well-being, my belief that there were well-meaning therapists out there. That wasn't enough to make me take that step to uncovering my past at that time, but it was enough to make me willing to find a therapist when I was ready to take that step in my early thirties.

The first therapist I saw in my thirties should not have been a therapist. I'm a firm believer that a therapist-patient relationship is as equally dependent on personality and compatible communication styles as a romantic relationship, and there is an essential understanding that differences are not necessarily a personal reflection. However, I still can't figure out why this person chose the mental health profession.

I saw her for about the last seven months of my pregnancy with my youngest daughter. My gut told me from the first day that I needed to find someone else, but I convinced myself that I was just trying to find an excuse to back out of therapy, so I continued to see her anyway, despite each session worsening my ability to cope with the issues that'd brought me to therapy in the first place. She was cold and dismissive, quick to tell me what my struggles were coming from without having any of my background, to instantly tell me I had "mommy issues" when I told her I wanted to talk about difficulties with my mother-in-law *before* I'd had a chance to tell her about my mother-in-law's abuse. As the weeks passed, I became more confused, convinced there was something seriously wrong with me, that I was not forgiving enough of those who'd abused me, and became more and more afraid of talking about anything of substance.

After I gave birth, I never went back to see her. For weeks, I decided that I was done with therapy, that I'd never try again, because I was emotionally in a significantly worse state than I had been and now had a new baby in the house, all the while battling those emotional challenges. I decided that I had been better off *before* I tried therapy and went back to trying to bury my trauma.

My second daughter was a few months old when I made the decision to try again. I'd just been on a vacation to the beach with my husband, my toddler and newborn, and my mother-in-law. During that week, I was in a sustained state of heightened anxiety, battling tears constantly, and couldn't seem to contain my outrage and disgust and anger and protective instincts when my mother-in-law kept telling blatant lies, changing facts from the past, and insisting on inappropriate comments and discussions, including proclaiming repeatedly that my toddler's Lego tower was phallic. My husband had grown up in this environment, and while he got frustrated with her because she wouldn't let the phallic commentary drop despite our repeated requests, he didn't think it was a big deal—he never had. I'd always struggled with being upset by things he was used to enduring, but I had previously clung to my convictions. Now, however, all I heard in the back of my mind was that I should let it go, that I just had "mommy issues."

therapy and a letter

I decided when we got home from that trip that I needed to return to therapy, that I needed to "fix" whatever was wrong with me so I could remove that tension from my marriage and keep from passing it down to my kids. I thought back to when I saw Joseph and used that experience to remind myself that good therapists were out there. I asked some local friends I knew were in therapy for recommendations and started there.

A woman that two of my friends saw had an appointment available several weeks out and I took it. Before that first day came, however, were two more incidents with my mother-in-law and I decided that even if it destroyed my marriage, something had to be done about it. My husband and I argued, then he finally agreed that *maybe* someone should talk to her about her sexual behaviors in front of our kids, but that he couldn't be that person; he couldn't do something he was certain would hurt his mother's feelings.

Which left *me*.

When I was young, I was physically abused by both of my biological parents and family on my dad's side, beat with hands, paddles, and belt buckles. I was punished with violence, beat unconscious by a large group of kids when I was barely eight years old for standing up for my sister. I'd been only feet away when a friend was viciously beat by her father when I was teen, and I'd been physically assaulted on multiple occasions by guys of various ages. Confrontation was something I avoided whenever humanly possible; my body literally felt like it was trying to kill me when I even thought about confronting someone.

I was scared—terrified, really—though I wasn't even sure of what. I just knew I couldn't sleep, couldn't stop shaking, was in a constant state of tunnel vision as the day for the confrontation neared. I was also furiously angry. Angry with my husband for not stepping up and setting boundaries with his mother, for not having a conversation that should have been coming from him. Angry that the reason he couldn't do that was because of how badly he'd been abused by her his whole life. Angry that he couldn't and didn't want to see that. Finally, I was filled with doubt; doubt that I could get the words out when the moment arrived, doubt that it would make any difference, doubt that I even should be having the conversation.

What if I was wrong? What if I really did just have "mommy issues" or was too sensitive about sexuality because of my history of sexual abuse and sexual assault? What if *she* was normal and *I* was wrongfully angry with her?

I'd had the date set for two days after my first therapy appointment with my new therapist. Regardless of every reason that had prompted me to seek therapy, I decided I had to hijack the first appointment to get help with how to handle the impending confrontation. I arrived, introduced myself, and told her that I needed help with an immediate problem. Ignoring all my mother-in-law's past abuse of my husband and me, I began only with the incidents I needed to include in the conversation in two days; most

therapy and a letter

recently, the phallic comments from the beach, the fact that after being alone with my oldest for two hours we came home to our barely two-year-old daughter rubbing her chest and saying "pretty," and that a week after that, my mother-in-law started stripping her clothes off in my living room in front of my kids and me.

My therapist listened, and the second I stopped speaking, she said, "Are you fucking kidding me?" After being prepared to hear that I was overly sensitive and overprotective, that my mother-in-law's behavior was normal and it was my concern that wasn't, it took me a while to process what I'd heard. In fact, I thought I'd imagined it at first. But then she said it again.

When it finally sank in that she'd actually said it, that my therapist was as indignant about the behavior as I was, I started laughing hysterically and sobbing. Over and over, I kept repeating, "I'm not crazy." I was in shock and realized just how deeply rooted those feelings of being crazy, the self-blame for everything around me ran.

Once I was able to calm down enough to stop laughing and crying, to carry on a conversation, my therapist patiently and nonjudgmentally guided me out of that place of guilt and self-blame and gave me the tools I needed to explain to my husband my mother-in-law's behavior—and the danger that posed for our children. And she showed me that my instincts had been there for a reason; I didn't merely have "mommy issues."

I went home and shared all my new knowledge and understanding with my husband. While he didn't understand it fully, he agreed to have the conversation with his mother himself. In the meantime, I wrote a letter to my mother-in-law that I shared with my therapist in another session. In the letter, I touched on the various types of abuse my husband and I suffered at her hands, the danger of what she was doing to our children, and how I was prioritizing my children by protecting them from her. Writing it was both difficult and cathartic.

My therapist was honest with me, wanting me to understand that if I ever decided to share the letter with my mother-in-law, she likely wouldn't change anything or even apologize. That she was more likely to get angry or simply excuse away everything she'd done, refusing to accept responsibility for her actions. That I should not let my healing or happiness hinge on her reaction to being confronted in that way.

I nodded and laughed nervously—there was no way in hell I'd ever send a letter like that to anyone, let alone my mother-in-law. That required a courage I didn't possess—it was too loud when I'd learned the hard way that silence was better, safer—both physically and emotionally.

Everyone processes trauma differently. For me, I tend to obsess at some point or another, and I was definitely in an obsession stage right then. I read and re-read and re-read and re-read that letter I wrote. Then started all over again. Each time I read through, I experienced all the emotions just as intensely—all the fear and self-loathing and confusion and pain and anger and hatred and shame. I wanted so desperately

therapy and a letter

to let those emotions go but couldn't figure out how to even begin with them held so tightly, so close, that I couldn't even breathe. I realized I needed to send that letter to her—that I had no choice. That in order to have the space to breathe and heal, I'd have to break my silence, show that I was no longer going to be held down, ensure that I could never again go back to that place of self-doubt and thinking I was crazy due to her abuse.

With my voice and hands trembling, I told my husband what I intended to do. I offered to let him read the letter first if he'd like (which he chose not to do), but I did not ask for his permission. Then, in an otherworldly moment in which I felt disembodied, as if I was watching myself from above, I read through the letter one last time and—with the thought that I could finally start to heal—I clicked send.

in-process

Brené Brown studies courage, vulnerability, shame, and empathy, and teaches through her writing, podcast, and TED talk (The Power of Vulnerability) about how those concepts function in our lives, as well as their relationship with one another. According to her, vulnerability requires courage, and we cannot experience connection without vulnerability. And if you really think about it, that makes perfect sense.

Think about experiences from your own life, those moments when you felt your deepest connection to another person, whether a romantic partner or a friend or a family member. It likely involved some level of vulnerability on both sides, as well as fear. The reason for that is because when we are vulnerable, we can be hurt in ways we can't if we remain closed off, and fear is both a normal and healthy response to the possibility of being hurt.

I always knew on an intellectual level that I'd have to move past that fear in order to come to terms with being vulnerable if I was going to be a writer—particularly if I was going to infuse anything from my own life into my writing and truly connect with my readers. I understood that sharing what I'd written with someone would mean accepting the possibility that it wouldn't be well-received, that a reader's reaction could be downright hurtful, whether intentional or not. Just as I'd acknowledged that tackling my memoir wasn't going to be easy.

Trying to sift through memories and determine which ones will make the cut and which won't when they all are part of who you've become would be a difficult feat for anyone, let alone someone with trauma to sift through. I've always admired people who had the strength and courage to accomplish something of that magnitude and then share their pasts with the world; the beautiful and the ugly, the inspiring and the abhorrent. Everyone's history includes some mix of good and bad because we are complex beings, and everyone has secrets. However, acknowledging this doesn't make facing—let alone sharing—those parts of yourself any easier.

"Not easy" was how I expected drafting my own memoir to be, but I was a bit misguided. Writing a painful memoir was one of the most difficult undertakings in my life. There was no way to take a shortcut or detour around the most distressful memories; I was forced to go back to every single harrowing experience in my life that I'd spent decades trying to forget existed and *relive* them as if they were happening all over again. And it turned out that no amount of advanced pep-talks to myself or reminders of the beautiful, healed state that would lie somewhere on the other side was sufficient preparation for reliving my past trauma.

At some point, I began drafting a chapter I'd been intentionally putting off; I just knew it was time. The chapter was about when I was raped by my boyfriend's brothers when I was thirteen. I wrote it and began a cycle of obsession over it, much like the one I'd gotten into when I wrote a letter to my mother-in-law about her abuse. I read and tweaked and read and tweaked the chapter for days and days on end, unable to even think about anything else. My heart was pounding and I was sweating profusely and shaking and having trouble breathing around the clock; my body was in a constant state of fear. Most nights I couldn't slow the racing in my mind enough to sleep, and when I could, my nightmares of old were waiting for me: nightmares about being chased and beaten and raped by groups of men, often while I called for my father to help me as he abandoned me to the predators. My eyelids would droop during the day in search of respite and instead I'd see the eyes of the oldest brother.

I researched disability leave at my firm daily, sure the only way I'd ever escape what I was experiencing was if I spent some time in an in-patient psych facility. One of my biological brothers had been in one when he was a teen, and he'd been on so many medications that he was a zombie—didn't even recognize my sister or me. I'd always been terrified of something like that happening to me after that experience, but I longed for it during this period, the relief from the constant physiological and emotional state of panic in which I was trapped.

Urges to engage in old self-harm habits returned with a vengeance, and it took every ounce of willpower I had to keep from giving in. When I got into a car for any reason, I began to picture myself being plowed into by another vehicle at a stoplight and think it wouldn't be so bad. Sometimes, I even imagined I would simply drive into oncoming traffic or into a guardrail at highway speed. It wasn't that I wanted to die, but I wanted—I *needed*—a reprieve.

In therapy, I mentioned that I was having trouble sleeping and that my normal self-care wasn't sufficient anymore. I explained that I'd written about my early teenage rape and couldn't seem to stop fixating on it. My therapist introduced me to the concept of retraumatization, and I knew immediately that's what was happening. But what to do about it? She was willing—encouraging even—of discussing the incident during our session, but that was territory I was nowhere near capable of traversing—I'd barely even written it down. Instead, I promised I'd give every effort to stop reading it, even if that meant I couldn't open my manuscript at all, until I was back to a normal state of functioning.

And I did sincerely give every effort, but failed day after day after day. I thought back to when I went live with my blog post on consent, the very first time I'd ever publicly referred to my early teenage rape as such and the most I'd ever discussed the events before I drafted that chapter of my memoir. A lot of the emotional burden with that post was similar to what I was currently experiencing and I remembered that after the post had been up for a while, having other people know a piece of my story brought a kind of relief I'd never before experienced.

I need to share this with someone, I thought. *Right now.*

Once that decision was made, though, I still had the challenge of figuring out who that someone would be. Even people who'd read my post may not have the same reaction to that part of my life story when all the detail had been laid out.

What if people blame me for what happened? What if people think it was my own fault for being there in the first place, for not trying to fight my way past the two brothers? What if they just think I was a slut like my friend and boyfriend did at the time?

I honestly wasn't sure if I could emotionally withstand a reaction of that sort. I've always been fairly self-aware, and exceedingly so since I started addressing my past years before I was facing this dilemma. I was very much aware that I was barely holding myself together, barely maintaining my sanity, barely keeping my suicidal ideation from progressing any further. But I also couldn't continue the way things were.

There were two women I'd met online since pursuing my writing career—both writers themselves—who'd been sources of support when I was faced with fear of putting myself out there. Two women who had been encouraging and kind and never once judged anything in our copious correspondence. I decided those women would be the people I'd trust with my story. Instead of pulling out just that one chapter, I sent to both of them everything I had drafted at that point, giving them a zoom lens into some of the most traumatic parts of my history. I queued up the emails, attached the drafts, took a deep, shaky, and tear-filled breath, and made myself vulnerable in a way I'd never been before.

After I clicked send, I wasn't sure I'd ever be able to breathe normally again. Ever be able to stop trembling, ever have my heart beat slow and steady rather than hammering rapidly against my chest. Self-doubt and gut-churning regret set in immediately, and I had a desperate wish to undo what I'd just done. My hypervigilance went into overdrive and my head was darting around at every tiny sound; I felt like I was trapped in a horror movie knowing I was next to die, but not exactly when or from where the fatal threat would come.

My daily routine involves an early bedtime because I rise well before the sun every morning to write. I knew I wouldn't get any sleep, but I forced myself to lie in bed anyway. Hours ticked by slowly as I stared at my darkened ceiling, my heart still trying to help me escape an invisible danger. I relived—over and over—my early teen rape, searching in desperation for anything I could have done to stop it, for any clue I might have secretly enjoyed the assault as my

in-process

boyfriend and close friend at the time had believed since I hadn't violently fought my aggressors.

Hot tears slid silently down my temples to soak my pillow as I imagined the end of my relationship with the two women to whom I'd sent my in-process manuscript. It was in those moments as I was trying to imagine my life without them part of it that I realized how important these two people I'd never met in person had become to me, how pivotal they were not just to my writing career, but to my healing journey.

How would I ever forgive myself if those relationships ended because of what I'd shared? How would I live with what had happened if they blamed me as my friend and boyfriend had back then? How would I ever recover my sanity if my fear of being disbelieved and dismissed came to pass?

At 4:30 am, the alarm on my phone sounded. Still awake, though groggy, I reached over and flipped it off as I climbed out of bed. After making coffee, I booted up my laptop, opened my email, and froze; there was an unread message from one of the women waiting for me. I stared at that line in my inbox without moving long enough that my screen went into sleep mode. The act of sliding my finger around on my trackpad and typing in my password anew brought me out of my stupor enough that this time I clicked on the email to open it.

As my eyes tore through the words on the screen, the nausea in the pit of my stomach grew before morphing unnoticed into tears and relief; a relief so intense I could scarcely breathe. A relief that far exceeded my fear since the night before and was excruciating in a way that rivaled some of the most heartbreaking moments in my life. My vulnerability had been met with compassion, kindness, and understanding. She thanked me for sharing my pain—for trusting her enough to do so—and she was vulnerable in return. She gave to me the words I'd never received before, the words I'd been struggling to give to myself and so desperately needed to hear from someone else.

She told me none of it was my fault.

As much as I'd obsessed over the chapter I wrote detailing my rape at the hands of my boyfriend's brothers, I obsessively re-read this email I'd received for days. I couldn't really figure out how to find words to respond, how to express that her email meant more to me than she could ever understand. That more than twenty years later, hearing the words I needed and should have heard back then was healing in a way I never expected.

Then I received the response from the second woman and no less compulsively re-read her words. She told me it was infuriating the way I'd been let down by so many people in my life. She told me I had a very important story to tell, that I would help so many others with similar experiences by sharing mine. She offered to help me as I progressed whenever and however I needed. I again struggled with finding words to convey how important her response was to me, how deeply smoothing for the jagged edges that experience had carved into me.

in-process

As the weeks passed, I stopped re-reading the emails from these two women. My heightened anxiety faded back to a more normal caliber and I returned to working on my manuscript, finally ready to tackle more from my past. At some point, the urge to re-read the chapter about my early teenage rape returned and I navigated to those pages. I read through my words, my account of what happened, and didn't have that same sense of impending doom I'd had before. I was still panicky, but not as severe. When I reached the last word, I thought about how difficult it had been to write that experience down, how difficult it had been to share it with the two women I'd sent it to. I thought about how much more at peace I was than I had been when the words first came pouring from my fingers.

I realized I'd given myself a gift, though I hadn't realized it at the time. By offering up my vulnerability, I'd accessed an extraordinary courage I hadn't realized I possessed and was establishing a precedent for the presence of *more* courage in my life. That courage was what I would need to heal myself. As much as I'd felt that I required the affirmation from someone else that fault for what happened didn't rest on my shoulders, what I'd really needed was to hear it from myself. And while I hadn't realized it at the time, the act of sharing that part of my life story with others, while uncertain of the outcome, was how I did that.

work variance

When I went back to college after a few years off, I was determined to "do things right." I'd been derailed during my freshman year by suddenly struggling ferociously in a subject that had always been easy for me and realizing my entire life's plan for my major and career was no longer a possibility. But I resolved to make sure that didn't happen again. Unlike my first college, which was a small liberal arts college, I was attending a large university with every course of study you could imagine.

I was encouraged by my foster mom and her sister to study accounting and pursue a CPA certification because there were always jobs in accounting and it had about the best job security of any professional career I could pursue. In my mind, I'd already proven that I couldn't make sound decisions and was more than happy to do what they suggested, declaring my major before I'd even taken a single accounting course. Luckily for me, it was a subject that made sense to me, fit in well with my severe over-achieving and Type A

moments of *extraordinary* courage

personality, and presented what I found to be a fun and interesting challenge.

I excelled in no small part out of an intense terror of failing; no matter what it took, no matter how hard I had to work, I could not allow myself to fail. And I had to do well enough to get a job offer at the end. In fact, when I was named the accounting student of the year at the end of my undergraduate degree and attended the awards ceremony, the department head introduced me by saying, "She isn't smarter than anyone else—she just works harder than everyone else." Of course, this back-handed compliment only reinforced my belief that if I didn't do *everything*, I wouldn't be worthy, desirable, successful.

After I graduated that year, I worked hard during an internship over the summer before returning to get my Master's degree. Shortly after my return, I received a job offer from the firm I'd interned with and accepted immediately; I didn't want to risk them realizing I wasn't as great as they thought and changing their mind. I was just intensely grateful to know I'd be employed once I finished my last year of schooling and took the exams to get my CPA; it was a bonus that it was such a great firm. From a corporate culture perspective, I truly believe they were the best of all the firms that recruited at my university, and that list of firms was considerable.

The next couple of years flew by in a blur of working exceedingly long days for weeks and months on end, showing up first and leaving last on top of several hours per day in commuting time. By my two-

work variance

year anniversary with the firm, I was officially burned out. My relationship with my husband was struggling because I was always in the office, even on weekends. And in late winter of that year, I'd discovered that the team I'd been working with since I started with the firm didn't care about me as a person like I'd thought.

I'd started having severe heart palpitations following a round of steroid medication and I was referred to a cardiologist when my physician couldn't determine what was happening. When I told my team that I'd have to miss part of a workday to see a cardiologist, I was told the timing was terrible and it would have to wait for a few weeks until it was more convenient. It was abundantly clear to me in that moment that my worth and my value on my team was tied only to how much work I produced every day.

After much discussion, my husband and I decided I needed to do something else within the firm, that I couldn't continue the way things were, so we decided to do a rotation overseas. A series of coincidences later, I instead remained in the US, pregnant with my oldest daughter and working from home in a different area of my firm. I was relieved to at least be able to cut out my commute; even though I worked significant overtime, I was able to spend more time with my husband. The work no longer relied upon the CPA I'd worked so hard to earn, but I didn't mind; I loved the diverting nature of a new challenge and everything I was doing was new to me.

Over the next several years, I was officially transferred to the area I'd been working in, the risk of returning to where I'd begun my career finally eliminated. I worked with a team that was highly intelligent, respectful, fun, and collaborative. And yet, as I began and then progressed along my healing journey, I felt a growing discord, though I desperately tried to banish it. How could I—a woman who'd spent her childhood living in a trailer without water or electricity and begging for money on the streets—have a right to feel discord with a career like the one I had? I felt I was ungrateful, and if I acknowledged it, I would no longer be of value to anyone and I would lose everything: the respect of my family, my financial security, the future I wanted for my children.

As much as I wanted to ignore it, however, the feeling simply grew until one day I could no longer ignore it and declared that I wanted to go back to what I'd loved and wanted to do in my heart my entire life, what I used to say I would do every time I answered that common ice-breaker question, "If you could do anything you wanted and money was not an issue, what would it be?"

I was going to write and edit books.

Pretty much the moment I made that declaration to my husband and my sister—after a hefty glass of wine—I started writing. And I haven't stopped. Those first months were feverish, as if all the writing I'd kept bottled up inside me for so long was bursting violently out of me. In a matter of months, I'd drafted six full-length novels, parts of several others, and taken notes on dozens of book ideas I simply didn't have the time to begin drafting. I realized when I paused to take a

work variance

breath that I'd never felt so alive. Writing is what my soul was born to do.

About a year and a half after I started writing again, I could no longer put off what I'd been avoiding even thinking about, simply tucking it back into a dark corner of my mind whenever the thought tried to pop out unbidden. I'd written all those books, I was furiously editing and working with beta readers, but I couldn't contract with a publishing company, I couldn't even self-publish a single book for so much as a penny without violating my employment contract with my firm. If I ever wanted to publish my books in any way, I would need to obtain formal permission from my firm: a work variance.

I did my research and knew there was paperwork to complete and multiple levels of approvals required before I would be in the clear. I had to demonstrate that there would be no conflict of interest if they provided approval. And the first person who had to agree that I'd done that was my manager.

I'd been working under her for several years already and considered her to be a friend, work aside. She was caring and respectful in ways my previous managers had not been. And yet, I was terrified to tell her that I wanted a variance to publish my books, to even tell her that I was writing them. I put it off as long as I possibly could, but the day came when I could put it off no longer.

Even so, I had many opportunities the day of my annual performance evaluation and clammed up, unable to speak, though I tried to will myself to do it.

What if I asked and she said no? What if I told her I was writing and she laughed? What if I lost my job simply because I made the request?

We met in person for the performance discussion, which—despite my fears every year that I'd in some way failed and let people down—was filled with praise. I smiled and nodded at appropriate intervals, but I was having trouble following everything she said, my eyes flitting around the room and out the window, looking everywhere except at her. My inability to make eye contact didn't go unnoticed and she questioned if I was okay, and asked me if there was anything I wanted to talk about. I opened my mouth and no sound came out. I shook my head no and got to my feet, looking at her for the first time. Her furrowed brow betrayed that she was concerned and that small detail gave me the spark of courage I needed to not give up on my dreams.

"Actually," I said as I looked away, my voice wobbling audibly as my vision tunneled, "there is something."

Then, I sat back down, took as deep a breath as I could manage, and began with the statement, "I love writing."

picture on the wall

During the gap year after my freshman year of college, I'd gotten married out of necessity. I loved my fiancé and one day expected to marry him, but we needed to live with his parents for a while and I wasn't allowed to stay if we didn't get married immediately, so his parents had dictated the timing, as well as everything else to do with the small wedding. And that was only the beginning.

Of course, I'd known that my new husband's parents were both abusive and that his step-father was a severe alcoholic—living with them wasn't ideal. But I didn't really have contact with anyone I'd been friends with in any capacity in high school; I had no close friends from my one year in college; my foster mom and I weren't on speaking terms since I'd moved out before my eighteenth birthday over a year earlier; and my younger sister still lived at home with our foster mom. Our choices had been slim: his parents or homeless. We'd chosen his parents, though there were many days I wondered if homeless would have been better—I knew the tiny trailer I'd lived in as a child without water or electricity would have been.

While we lived there in their basement in the excrement from my mother-in-law's fifteen cats, we were responsible for a very long list of chores, home maintenance activities, and significant portion of the home's expenses. At the time, I felt that my father-in-law was punishing my husband for his teen rebellion and my mother-in-law—who was about as fiscally irresponsible as you can imagine—was simply trying to make sure the bills she was responsible for got paid after she'd "accidentally" spent the money for them each month. And really, both of these likely played a role, but years later, after a lot of reflection and therapy and research into my in-laws' toxic behavior, I think it was primarily by design to keep us stuck there. Each month left us financially in the hole, beholden to them with a sheet of paper tallying the additional money we owed them and ensuring we didn't have even a cent to spend in a way we chose; my belief is only strengthened when I think back to how they eventually loaned us money to get a tiny apartment not far down the road but had staunchly refused to loan us a fraction of that money when we were going to use it for me to return to college at the end of my year off.

My father-in-law traveled for work; he was out of town during the weekdays and returned for the weekends. When he was home, the tension and anxiety already present skyrocketed. He smiled and made jokes and laughed, but only if things were exactly as he expected, the food he liked was prepared for him and served, he was never without an alcoholic beverage in his hands and a movie he chose running twenty-four hours a day in the background. His jokes were overtly sexual or harsh criticism. And when things didn't go his way, the entire house shook with the vibrations from his booming voice. He seemed to grow taller and broader, his face turning red, and every insecurity was attacked until you felt unworthy to be the floorboards under his feet.

My mother-in-law catered to his every whim when he was home, made equally-uncomfortable sexual jokes and innuendos, engaged in discussions with him about sex and sexual organs in front of us, trying to pull us into the conversation. As they had since I'd met them when I was young, they had sex loudly while we were in the next room and then talked about it afterwards.

During the weeks while he was gone, she had the same sexual inappropriateness, but her anger came out with more frequency and was unpredictable; often, something she found to be a compliment only hours before was suddenly an unforgivable insult. She'd fly into unexpected rages, screaming into our faces and calling us every name under the sun. She'd throw things at us—whatever was within arm's reach—and then blame us for making her angry when those things broke. She'd wake us in the middle of the night to do things like split wood, refusing to let us in the house until we'd done as she instructed. And any time I tried to reason with her, she kicked me out for some period of time. Living there was to be in a constant state of uncertainty, fear, and anxiety, and while I had moments of defiance where I rebelled against what was happening, primarily driven by seeing the unfairness and abuse my husband simply accepted—it was all he'd ever known—I learned to keep my head down and my mouth shut, to make myself as small and quiet as I possibly could when either of my in-laws flew into a rage. Especially my father-in-law, whose explosive temper not only terrorized me emotionally, but created a deep fear of physical violence from him as well; I knew he'd physically abused my husband when he was young.

We'd been there for about eight months when my mother-in-law decided one weekday that she wanted a picture hung in the living room and asked my husband to hang it for her. He refused, knowing as we all did that it was something that would set off my father-in-law, who wanted his childhood home to remain decorated the way it had been when he was growing up. But my mother-in-law wouldn't take no for an answer and argued with my husband, swearing that my father-in-law had given permission for her to hang it, and then screaming that her own son didn't love her enough to hang a picture; that if he loved her, he would do it. I attempted to interject, but was cut off by my mother-in-law, and my husband caved and hung the picture after asking her one more time to promise she'd gotten my father-in-law's blessing to do so.

When my father-in-law arrived home that weekend, he stopped short in the living room, staring at the newly-hung picture. Before he even said a word, my body flooded with dread. My vision tunneled and

picture on the wall

my stomach churned, my muscles felt tight and poised to flee and my breathing shallowed. It was as if the air in the room had suddenly drained away.

He asked about the picture, his voice indicating calm, though everything else about him betrayed his anger; his stance, the clenching of his jaw, the way he couldn't take his eyes from the picture.

Without a second's delay after my father-in-law's question, my mother-in-law pointed her finger at my husband and said, "He did it. I told him not to, but he did it anyway."

My jaw dropped and hung there, limp for a moment. I'd figured out long ago that she was a serial liar, making up allergies and illnesses and then changing them daily to garner sympathy from those around her. I'd realized how she'd twist facts to cast herself in a more positive light because I'd seen it happen enough times in the nearly decade I'd known her. Despite all this, I was caught off-guard by what had just happened. In every thought about my mother-in-law, every moment of anger and disgust, I'd never expected she'd direct a violent man's anger toward her own son, let alone for something she was responsible for and she'd lied to him about. It felt as if I'd just seen someone prove that two plus two equaled something other than four. All the arguments I'd had with my husband about her behavior—his defense of her that she was doing her best and really loved him—ran through my mind rapid-fire; that was the moment I realized he believed a lie. I was no expert on *non*-dysfunctional family dynamics, but there wasn't a person on the planet who could convince me that you could intentionally put into harm's way an innocent person you loved.

As my shock at what she'd just done wore off, my realization about her settling heavy on my heart, my chest filled with anger and indignation and supplanted my instinctive fear. Everything else in my body was screaming for me to make myself small, to silently backstep out of the room unnoticed and hide until everything passed, to keep myself safe and out of the focal point of the fight; I'd had nothing to do with hanging that picture, after all—it wasn't my battle to fight. But my heart refused to let me abandon my husband. I understood more than I ever had the extent of how he'd been abused and brainwashed, and he deserved to have someone stand up for him. I knew it was futile, that I wouldn't actually accomplish anything, but that didn't matter; what mattered was standing up for what was right simply because that was the right thing to do, and the *only* thing I could do when I loved my husband.

"That's bullshit!" I shouted at her, effectively pulling everyone's attention to me. "You're lying! I can't believe you're saying that! He said no, but you *swore* you'd gotten permission!"

The situation devolved into chaos, everyone yelling at everyone else, and my mother-in-law came toward me, hate and rage painted on her face. She called me every name I'd ever heard of and kicked me out of the house, pursuing me to the front door and then locking it behind me. As I always did when she kicked me out—

which happened not infrequently—I walked next door and sat on the neighbor's porch while he sat with me. It was after I relayed the story to him that I broke down and cried, overwhelmed by all the fear and anxiety I'd locked up during the confrontation. But I regretted nothing about having broken the silence surrounding me and spoken the truth.

eighty bucks

Before I entered foster care, most of my positive memories—the ones during which I felt safe and loved and optimistic—involved my mom playing her flute. I called them flute days; they were the days she was unlikely to yell at us or spank us, when she was more likely to hug and cuddle us. When I entered foster care, I carried with me an intensely positive and comforting association with the sound of that particular instrument, so when my foster mom asked my sister and me what instruments we were interested in learning to play, I immediately chose the flute. Once it was apparent that I wasn't going to change my mind, my foster mom returned my rented flute to the music store and bought me my very own brand-new flute.

I was flabbergasted by the gesture and couldn't believe something so nice was actually mine. As I developed my skill at playing the instrument, I took care of it, making sure it was cleaned after each use and polished occasionally. When the keys needed to be repadded or tightened, I took my flute to the local instrument repair shop to have it serviced, happily using my own money to do so once I started working at age fourteen.

From extensive use, the finish had worn off in a few spots that received the most contact when I was playing, leaving behind a noticeable pinkish hue. When I entered high school and played in the pit orchestra and marching band, several of my bandmates were upgrading to newer and better instruments. They were new and shiny and could produce a quality of sound my flute never could and never would, and I considered from time to time whether I should use the money I was saving from my job to buy a new instrument, but I never did. I couldn't go through with it; it felt like a betrayal to replace my beloved instrument. Memories of learning to play, of the sudden appearance of a deep vibrato when I started playing with my eyes closed, simply feeling the music and those wonderful emotions I'd had when my mom had played when I was little, of the astounding joy in my heart when my foster mom first gave it to me and assured me it was *mine*... they kept me tethered the flute I already had.

Throughout the next couple of years, my flute followed me, even when many of my belongings were left behind. It was one of the first things I grabbed when I stormed out of my foster mom's house a few months before my eighteenth birthday. It was carefully packed into the middle of my duffel bag of clothes when I drove from Virginia to Minnesota to start my freshman year of college, and again when I made the trek back to Virginia a year later. It was in an open-

eighty bucks

topped box carefully cradled on the floorboards of my little Mazda Protégé so it couldn't fall and get banged up when my husband and I left his parents' house for our own apartment a little over a year after that. My flute was much more than an instrument to me; it was a part of who I was.

After my husband and I had been on our own in an apartment for less than a year, we were struggling and failing to make ends meet while not only paying our own living expenses, but also trying to pay off the tab of debts his stepfather kept while we lived there in addition to the monstrous medical bills from two different hospitals and an emergency plastic surgeon related to an accident I'd been in shortly before we moved. Of course, we'd had no health insurance, and even with one ER doctor forfeiting his fees, we owed over thirty thousand dollars.

We both picked up extra jobs, even though my husband was vehemently against me doing so—I was in a lot of pain from the accident that would take years to finally taper off entirely. At one point, I was working three jobs with about four hours per day allotted to bathing, eating, and sleeping. My husband wasn't faring much better with his two demanding jobs. And still we were unable to even catch up financially. Things worsened when our minds and bodies suddenly could handle no more and we each had to give up a job. In an ever-constant state of trying to figure out how to make ends meet, I realized I had greater income potential if I left my hourly job and picked up extra shifts at my waitressing job. That change meant I only had that single source of income when my husband left that restaurant to cook somewhere else and they retaliated by firing me later that day.

I imagine my application made me look unreliable with the number of different jobs I'd had over the course of the last few years and that's why not one place called me back. I'd applied at gas stations, convenience stores, fast-food restaurants... everything and anything that had an application I could complete. I also tried to file for unemployment, but the restaurant claimed I was let go for poor performance. While I knew from every performance evaluation I'd received that what they said was a lie, I didn't have a copy of those evaluations to prove it, so I was denied unemployment.

It wasn't long before our bank account was empty—we had about thirty cents. Half a tank of gas. No food. And a tall stack of bills that were due. My husband was working in his new job, but wouldn't get his first check for another couple of weeks. We'd been counting on my tips to let us skate by to that date.

After pacing our tiny apartment while Joe was working, analyzing our situation from different angles, willing to consider anything to help, I came up empty-handed. I was out of ideas. A black case caught my eye as I paced and I stopped to stare at it.

My flute.

The thought made me feel more nauseous than I already was, but I didn't have a choice. My hands shook violently as I gently lifted my flute from where it was lying, placed it on my lap and flipped the case open. For long minutes, I feathered my fingers over the keys as

eighty bucks

memories paraded through my mind. The moment my foster mom had bought it for me, concerts and competitions and performances and practices. Holding it in my hands in sixth grade band class the first time I saw the boy who was now my husband. I loved that flute as much as an object could be loved and the thought of selling it felt like a piece of me was being ripped out. But I had to do it anyway, so I inhaled sharply, closed the lid, and rushed out the door to my car. Now that I'd decided what had to be done, I didn't see any point in delaying it.

Despite my attempts to banish my emotions since there was nothing I could do about the situation I was in, I was crying as I walked into the local music shop.

"I can give you sixty dollars for it," the owner said quietly.

I stared into his aged and wrinkled face after he spoke, into his eyes that seemed to reflect some of the grief I was feeling. I could tell he already understood, but explained anyway how special the instrument was to me, how intensely desperate I was, or I never would have even considered getting rid of it. The way the man's mouth pulled in at the sides told me he was moved by my emotional display, and he explained kindly that he could give me eighty dollars, but that was the most he could do as he'd already be selling it at a loss for that price.

I stared at those four twenty-dollar bills for a long time after I got back to my apartment, thinking about how much money we needed and how that eighty dollars meant nothing, how it really wouldn't even help. Thinking about how I'd surrendered a possession that was so much more than a physical object to me for four measly pieces of paper and wasn't really in any better a position. I felt like I'd lost a part of myself, that I'd betrayed myself and my foster mom, and that I'd just proven that I was a worthless failure.

As I cried, I tried to figure out how I'd screwed up so badly in my life, how I'd made so many poor decisions that I'd ended up in a situation where I had to pawn my most treasured possession. I thought about how hard I'd fought against ending up exactly where I was right then and knew with a certainty in my gut that soon it would be too late to ever escape the downward spiral I was trapped in. The thought of admitting to anyone that I had failed—that I needed help—was excruciating. That admission would mean formalizing how I'd let down every person who at some point had believed in me, believed in my ability to overcome the circumstances I was born into and succeed in life. While the situation would be no different, speaking the words out loud would sever any ability for me to delude myself.

Not only that, but I would be at someone else's mercy, utterly vulnerable. What if I was hurt worse than I already was? What if I admitted I'd messed up and asked for help and was denied? It would be better to never ask and never know for sure than to ask and be rejected… or was it?

There was no hope if I didn't ask, that much was certain. And while I may not get the help I needed, there was only a chance I would if I admitted I needed

eighty bucks

it and asked. My chest was caved in and my hands shaking in big jerky movements as I reached for my phone and dialed. With each ring, I considered hanging up; I wasn't sure I could follow through. And then my foster mom answered and I was out of time—I had to make a decision right then.

With a sharp intake of breath and a sob, I pushed the words out from between my lips.

"I need help."

rabbit

Shortly after I started writing again, I was chatting with my new neighbor and she asked me what I did for a living. I told her I was a CPA and worked in public accounting in audit support (my day job) and then I asked what she did. She told me she was a graphic designer and gave me her website so I could check her out, which I did before tucking away that tidbit of information. I was early in those months of feverishly drafting my first fiction novels (the Life Imperfect series), so I wasn't ready to start thinking about cover design yet, but I knew I would be at some point.

Over the next few months, my husband and I learned that our neighbors had attended the same college we did when we went back to school, only a handful of years earlier than we did. They told us they met while they were there and asked how we met; we told them in band class in sixth grade and they balked, as people often do, unsure what to say in response. They looked at our kids and asked if they were both mine; I'm mixed, so I have tan skin, dark brown eyes, and dark curly hair while my youngest daughter has a fair complexion, neon blue eyes, and bleach-blonde hair. I laughed and explained that while my husband's hair is now a medium brown in color and his eyes are more gray than blue, his hair and eyes were the same color as our daughter's until his late teens. Our neighbors shared that once a year they get together and do a weekend camping trip on an old college classmate's property with about fifty of their friends from college and asked if we did anything like that. We told them no, that we went back to college as adults much older than most of our classmates and we commuted forty miles each way to attend while working full time, so we didn't really fit in with college culture; we are really only close with two people we met while we were there.

Each conversation left me more hesitant than the prior one to answer questions because our responses were unusual and unexpected. We left our neighbors visibly surprised—their eyebrows raised, their jaws dropping slightly, their eyes darting away, their words suddenly changing the subject—and that left me feeling like an outcast as well as battling guilt that I was the source of their obvious discomfort.

A little over a year after we moved in, I started talking to my husband about the cover for my book. I knew I needed to find someone to help me, but felt completely lost about how to get started. I had done research—too much of it, so I was left with so many options and conflicting advice that my head was spinning. I found a site to use to solicit quotes from graphics professionals, but I wasn't confident I wouldn't be scammed, something I read about happening often in the world of indie authors. I remembered that my neighbor was a graphic designer, but kept dismissing the idea as soon as it popped up; asking her for a quote would mean telling her I was also a writer and that was something I hadn't done yet outside a small circle of family and very close friends. It was a big deal to do that; for me, once I've said something out loud, I can't *not* follow through and I *won't* fail. Speaking the words implies a confidence on my part, and that was something I didn't have much of at that point in my life.

During one of our conversations, my husband brought it up and suggested I ask our neighbor for a quote. I knew it was a good suggestion, but it was an uncomfortable idea. I was even embarrassed about my hesitation to ask, about my lack of confidence in myself, so I couldn't find a way to explain why *not* asking the neighbor was a good idea, and finally agreed—*out loud*—to ask her if mine was the kind of project she'd be interested in the next time I saw her.

It actually took until the fourth time I saw her, but I did finally dredge up enough gumption to tell her that I was writing a book I was planning to publish and would be looking for a cover designer—had she ever designed a book cover before? She told me she hadn't, but that she was comfortable foraying into that territory, provided me a link to her portfolio, and asked me to send her the detailed cover requirements via email, which I did that evening.

Before I'd gotten her quote back, I saw her outside doing spring gardening and she said she had something for me, asking me to hold on for a moment. She ran into her house and came back with a book in her hand.

"I just finished this book," she said. "It was really good and I know you like to read, so I thought you'd enjoy it. Are you familiar with her?"

I accepted the proffered book and read the cover. *Rabbit* by Patricia Williams. "No, I'm not," I replied.

"She's a comedian and this is her memoir. I know you mentioned in your email about your book that you had a tough childhood and so did the author. But you'll be laughing the whole time because she's so funny in the way she talks about everything. It's good. Borrow it and return it whenever you're done."

"Okay, thanks," I said.

I smiled, but my heart was racing and my breathing was labored. I appreciated that she remembered I said I loved to read and that she was loaning me a book she thought I'd enjoy, but being reminded that I'd written in my cover requirements that the book was personal to me because of some shared experiences with the story made me feel panicky. I didn't normally share that kind of information with people—let alone people I didn't know really well.

That night, I started the book. And sure enough, I laughed out loud during the introduction; the author has a very engaging way of communicating. I've never

rabbit

seen or heard her comedy, but I could definitely hear her voice in her words as I read. By the time I'd gotten through the first chapter, I was convinced it was a book my husband would enjoy, though he's more of a book-on-tape kind of person. I read him the introduction and the first chapter, he agreed that he'd like to hear the rest of it, and we grabbed him an audiobook copy he could listen to during his commute to and from work each day.

As life does sometimes, it got crazy and I wasn't able to do my nightly reading for several days, so my husband progressed through the book much faster than I did. He was somewhere in the latter half when he got home from work one evening—I hadn't progressed past the third chapter yet—and was visibly agitated.

"Don't read any more of that book," he said right away.

"What do you mean?" I asked, confused. I knew he'd been enjoying the author's gift for storytelling.

"Don't read it. Or at least skip chapter five, but I know you and I don't think you can just skip part of it, so stop reading it."

"Not finishing something is as bad as skipping it for me," I laughed. "You know that."

"I'm serious," he said without a hint of humor mirrored in his voice. "You shouldn't read it."

My heart skipped at the gravity in his voice and I flashed back to the introduction; the author had said that she was going to talk about things she'd never told anyone before, not even her husband, and then said she should probably warn him about chapter five.

Thoughts of what would prompt someone to write that flew through my mind rapid-fire, mixing with the urges inside to finish the book because I hate leaving things unfinished. Ultimately, I decided I needed more information from my husband to make a decision.

"What happens?" I asked.

He looked me straight in the eyes, holding my gaze for a moment as I saw moisture begin pooling in his. "She's raped. As a child. Don't do this to yourself."

Everything stopped for a moment as my history flashed through my mind. The thought of any of those things happening to other little girls, even if they were now adults, was more than my lungs could handle for a moment as my chest caved in and my eyes filled with tears, too. I nodded.

"Okay," I said. "I won't finish it right now and I'll go ahead and give it back. Maybe one day I'll be able to read it."

Once I made the decision to not finish the book, though, I couldn't touch it save to move it from one side table to another. I'd approach, stop in front of it, then just stare at the cover. Part of me felt like it was a test of my progress healing and that not reading that chapter meant I was failing that test. The other part of me was at peace that I wasn't yet to a place in my healing journey where I could read about what happened to her. Slowly, that first part of me faded away until I was almost entirely at peace.

Yet, I *still* couldn't pick up that book to return it to my neighbor.

rabbit

Every day for months, I told myself to take the book next door and return it; I'd had it significantly longer than it was kosher to borrow a book from someone, and the more time that passed, the more embarrassing it was that I still had it. When I saw my neighbor outside, my body filled with dread that she might inquire about the book, how I liked it.

What would I say?

I realized my apprehension of her bringing up the book every time I saw her was rooted in the same fear that kept me from just picking it up and giving it back to her to begin with: I had no idea what to tell her when she inevitably asked if I liked it. Rules of politeness indicated I should just say yes and do my best not to elaborate—perhaps by changing the subject. In this way, I would avoid making my neighbor uncomfortable by explaining—even without any level of detail—that I hadn't been able to finish the book and why.

But that whole concept irked me on a fundamental level—it always had. Lying as good manners? I'd rejected that idea since I could remember. People would respond, "It's not lying, it's being polite," but whether it was called polite or not didn't change the fact that it was lying. As an adult working to address my childhood trauma, I saw it as a dangerous societal norm, this expectation to lie about anything unpleasant—no matter how true—being expected in polite society. However unintentional, the underlying message is to keep your pain and your truth to yourself, and that dishonesty is valued over discomfort and conversation that isn't comprised solely of superficial pleasantries. No wonder so many people with any kind of struggle in life, regardless of source, feel so alone. No wonder it's so common to lie and feel no remorse for it.

Of course, I was also working—*hard*—to stop keeping everything I felt locked up inside. I was working to accept all the parts of me, and part of self-acceptance is not hiding yourself. Part of my journey was to break the silence I'd battled for so long and I knew I'd have to be honest when I had the conversation with my neighbor in order to remain true to myself.

But, *damn*, I didn't want to—I just wanted to avoid the conversation altogether. Every interaction I'd had with her or her husband had left me feeling less like them and less accepted for who I am, each conversation with them or other neighbors making it ever-more obvious that my husband and I were... different from the other folks in our neighborhood, in both simple and innocuous as well as fundamental ways. But this was the neighborhood we'd chosen to live in—not for ourselves, but for our children—so it was imperative we not alienate our neighbors.

The chill of early fall was in the air in the mornings, the afternoons no longer hot, but comfortably warm and sunny, and the leaves on the trees were beginning their vibrant autumn display when I finally stood in front of the side table holding the book. I stared down at it for a moment, took a deep breath, and grabbed it; it was time. I'd had it for an absurdly long time and needed to return it, no matter what that meant. Even if I had to tell a social lie, I couldn't keep the book in my house for another day.

rabbit

My hands shook, my heart raced painfully, my legs threatened to buckle, and I was sweating like it was the middle of the summer again as I started down the street; I knew I'd see my neighbor at the bus stop where we both waited for our kids to get home from school every afternoon. I also knew she was usually there early—like me—so there was a good chance none of the other parents would be there yet.

As I rounded the corner, I saw my neighbor, but she wasn't alone as I'd expected. That day, there were several other parents already there and more heading down the street. It turned out everyone had chosen to head over early for a few extra minutes to enjoy the beautiful weather. But it meant I would now have an audience when I returned the book.

Crap.

As I approached, I attempted to keep the book hidden to my side and mentally crossed my fingers that she wouldn't notice until we were walking back to our houses and I could just hand it to her as I continued along to my house listening to the chatter of my oldest daughter as she told me about how kindergarten was that day.

"Oh, you've got the book," she said with a wave as I slowed near the curb.

My stomach bottomed out and everything began to spin at her greeting; it would be a miracle if I made it through the next several minutes without bursting into flames or passing out from dizziness and lack of oxygen. *Why can't I just be normal?*

"Yep," I said, trying to force a smile. "Sorry I've had it for so long."

"Oh, that's fine," she replied. "I already read it. I'm going to loan it to a few others who want to read it next."

I nodded and held it out to her. "Thank you for loaning it to me."

She accepted the book and I hoped it wasn't damp from all the sweat drenching my hands. I knew I had a very tiny window of time to speak again and change the subject before she asked the question I knew was on her mind, but my body was uncomfortably frozen and I couldn't even make my jaw cooperate; I stood there in mute silence staring awkwardly at my neighbor, my eyes just... stuck.

"So, what did you think of it? She's funny, right? She talks about all these horrible things but you're laughing about it." She paused to laugh as if she was remembering something from the book as she glanced down at it for a moment. Then her eyes returned to me. "Did you like it?"

I swallowed dryly. "I liked what I read of it—you're right that she's funny," I replied, my voice small and quiet.

My neighbor's brows drew together and she tilted her head. "Oh... you didn't finish it? Do you need more time? You're welcome to borrow it until you're done."

I could understand her confusion—it was a short book and I'd had it for months. How could I possibly not have had time to finish it?

rabbit

My head shook quickly. "No, I didn't. I can't right now." *Please leave it at that,* I begged silently.

Instead, she held the book toward me. "Take your time—just return it after you're done."

I shook my head again. "No, it's not that."

Finally my eyes cooperated and tore away from her face to dart around for a moment before settling on my feet. Right then, I wished I'd just lied and said the book was great. Then I wouldn't be standing there feeling like my body was going to kill me, making a spectacle in front of the neighborhood parents. But there was no turning back time and changing my response. Besides, was that really what I wanted? I'd been fighting to step out of the silence; this was just another opportunity, even if it was one that I wasn't ready for.

I let out my breath slowly and forced my eyes to lift to hers.

"My husband got it on audiobook and listened faster than I could read it. He told me I shouldn't read part of it, that it would be too triggering for me, so I haven't been able to finish it. Maybe another time."

Her eyebrows drew even closer than they already were, and she gave a small shake of her head; she was clearly having difficulty understanding. "Triggering?" she asked.

"Yeah," I said, my eyes darting away; I couldn't keep eye contact any longer. At least not while I said the next few words. "He said chapter five has similarities to my own past, things I'm not sure I can handle reading about right now."

There was a beat of silence. "Oh. Wow. Okay... wow. Um... well... I guess..."

I went into make-her-comfortable mode, assuring her it was totally fine, that it wasn't a big deal, that I was sorry I'd made her uncomfortable. I focused on the author's storytelling manner in the first chapters that I *had* read. I babbled until the bus pulled up to the curb, saying anything I could think of to put her at ease until she could—politely—exit the conversation.

Later that evening, I was furious with myself for how I'd behaved in response to my neighbor's discomfort, for belittling myself and my experiences because she wasn't sure how to respond. While I didn't have the intent to make her uncomfortable, it also wasn't my responsibility that she was. Just as it wasn't my responsibility or my fault that she didn't know how to respond; no more than it was my fault that I'd been abused and assaulted in my past.

But then I remembered something I'd written in *Finding Annie*, a piece of advice I come back to often; while it's true and I'm the one who wrote it, I sometimes forget and then focus on the wrong thing:

> "The journey [...] had always reminded me more of one of the steep mountain roads that surrounded our secluded little valley. You moved slowly back and forth along the switchbacks that might seem to be taking you back the way you came, and might seem to be endless, making no real progress toward the top of the mountain. But really, if you just

backed up far enough to see the whole road, you'd realize you were always advancing incrementally with each pass. And the winding road itself, if you just took a moment to notice, was at least as beautiful as the view from the top."

I may have slipped into prioritizing someone else's comfort over my own, but that had only happened because I'd first broken the silence I'd been trapped in for months and spoken the truth. And *that* was progress; progress I should be proud of.

remember when...

When I was in my mid-twenties, my husband and I were both attending college full-time and working full-time alongside our studies. We lived a good hike from where we were attending school, but it meant we were living rent-free—the only requirement was that we helped with yard upkeep throughout the year, which we were more than happy to do. It seemed our lives had finally started to turn around and we were moving full-steam ahead in the opposite direction we'd been speeding toward for much of our lives.

Even with a bright future on the horizon, I was struggling with addictions; some obvious, like excessive alcohol consumption and chain-smoking, and some not, like near-starvation and purging with Miralax if I ate even a bite more than I'd allotted myself. I convinced those who noticed the rapid weight loss that it was entirely due to healthy eating habits (which I didn't have) and exercise (which I was doing compulsively). For a while I had a sudden resurgence of my childhood nightmares again, the ones where I

moments of *extraordinary* courage

was chased and raped, which contributed to worsening alcohol and nicotine dependencies in an effort to take the edge off.

One day, a new compulsion arrived seemingly out of nowhere. I woke up and decided I had to find my biological family. My biological sister had been with me since she and I entered foster care, but my parents had disappeared not long after our removal from their care and we'd lost track of my older brothers once they turned eighteen. I spent hours for days and weeks on end combing through public records and websites in an effort to locate even a single family member. Eventually, I came to the conclusion that I would have to figure out which online service was legitimate in their claimed capability to locate people and not going to scam me if I devoted some precious, hard-earned money for the task to reconcile with my past. My dollars were focused on the future now—I'd been saving for the day my husband and I finished college and needed to get a place of our own wherever our new jobs took us.

After some discussion with my husband on which site to trust, I input my check card information and waited, feeling sick and as if I might pass out, as the system processed my first name request. Minutes later, I had results for that person. A few days and payments to a couple of other search sites later, I had information for my two brothers and my father. My mother, on the other hand, seemed to have not only disappeared from Social Services before I was even ten years old, but from all public records. (It was over ten years later,

remember when...

when my sister had her DNA analyzed through an ancestry company, that we discovered my mother had died when we were in our late teens from complications related to severe alcohol poisoning.)

My brothers were both incarcerated in separate state prisons for multiple violent offenses, such as assault with a deadly weapon, firing on police officers, breaking and entering, and assault with the intent to kill. Reading the charges felt like I was reading about other people; I couldn't reconcile what the screen relayed with the two obnoxious older brothers I'd had when I was little. I scribbled down their addresses and decided to write them both letters.

My dad, while his historical facts showed several periods in which he'd been incarcerated as well—the first of which I already knew about from many years before—it showed he was currently living about an hour away in one of the many cities I'd lived in with him as a child. And right there on the screen was a phone number.

An actual phone number.

I stared at the digits, remembering the last time I'd heard his voice. It was the month before my tenth birthday, eighteen months after I'd entered foster care. The call had lasted less than a full minute. He'd called to tell my sister and me that our grandmother—his mother—had died. He'd said he couldn't talk, that he loved my sister and me, and would call again soon.

He'd never called back.

My mind flashed rapid-fire back to all the moments I'd written letters to him over the years as I grew up—

letters I knew would never be delivered to him, letters he'd never get to read. I remembered all the nights I'd cried in bed, missing him and wondering why he'd never called us again.

Memories I'd had locked up tightly for years seeped out from their dusty corners; memories of his belt buckle making me bleed when I was being punished, his laughter when I was scared of horror movies and certain men in our lives. Memories of my confusion when he dropped my sister and me off for a weekend visit with our mom and never came back. And, of course, my memory of telling him how my teenage cousin had touched me against my will and threatened to hurt me if I told anyone when I was not quite seven. How my dad had yelled at me, called me a liar, and made me promise I'd never tell anyone else.

It was a few days before I could manage to dial the number I'd found, my hands shaky whenever I looked at it, my breath and heart stalling painfully. It had been thirteen years since I'd spoken to him, fourteen since I'd last seen him, and yet my body felt like I'd been thrust back in time, feeling the pain of missing him so intensely all over again.

What if he didn't want me in his life anymore? What if I called and he didn't want to hear from me? What if he'd moved on and never even thought of me anymore? I wasn't sure I could continue to breathe if that happened.

Eventually, I called the number and held my breath as it rang. After a while, a voicemail picked up and I left an awkward message in which I stuttered profusely; it would be a miracle if whoever listened on the other end could unravel what I'd been trying to say.

After about a week of compulsively checking that my phone was not in silent mode, checking the volume of my ringer, having my phone a permanent fixture in my hand, he called one night. I suspected it was him, though I didn't recognize the number. I answered, and his voice came over the line, using the nickname he'd called me as a child.

"Daddy?" the word rushed from my mouth with my breath, and then I started bawling. I couldn't believe that after all those years I was actually having a phone call with my father. I berated myself silently for using such a childish word to address him—I was an adult, "Dad" would have been more appropriate—but it had rushed out before I could even think.

We spoke for a long time and agreed to have another call soon. That call turned into another and another, and then an in-person visit. The experience was surreal and I couldn't stop grinning, though I was so anxious I'd fantasized about just running away from my life before he arrived, unsure I could handle seeing him in person. But I didn't, and we visited, setting a date for another get together.

When I was younger, I'd fantasized about finding my dad again one day, about telling him that he'd been wrong. In my fantasy, my dad would tear up, he would look me in the eye, and he would tell me he was sorry. He would tell me he should have believed me, that he wished he had. I would tell him how I'd struggled my whole life because of what happened, and he'd explain to me why he'd suddenly not believed me when he'd always defended my honesty, why he'd made me swear never to tell another person. I'd tell him that I told my mother and that I felt guilty for breaking my promise to him, and he'd tell me he was glad I did, that he never should have forced me to make the promise. He would tell me that he was wrong and that my cousin never should have touched me. That it wasn't my fault it had happened, that it wasn't my fault I couldn't stop it, and that it wasn't my fault that he hadn't believed me. He would help me to understand how circumstances for him could have been so bad that he'd treated me that way and ask for my forgiveness and I'd give it to him. He'd tell me that he loved me, that he always had, through everything that happened.

All those fantasies came crashing back when it had been about six or eight weeks of frequent contact and I could no longer even talk to him anymore without hearing him calling me a liar about my cousin. I spent every waking moment obsessing over that event, both what my cousin had done to me and my dad's reaction when I told him; I couldn't focus on anything else. Not my marriage, not my job, not my classes. Nothing. I knew something had to give, and I got so lost in my childhood fantasies about my father feeling and expressing remorse and sorrow over what happened that I didn't immediately discard the notion of telling him when it materialized in my mind.

No one knew I'd decided to bring it up with my dad; I was too afraid to bring up something I'd barely even told anyone about, too afraid to admit to anyone that I was still so devastated about something that had happened so long ago, and too afraid of saying I would do something I felt was likely I'd chicken out of doing when the time came to follow through. My body entered a near-constant state of feeling panicked; I spent days unable to sleep or eat anything at all, days not being able to take a full breath or look around without feeling dizzy, days of sweat pouring from every part of my body, even though I was frequently so cold I was shaking, so that I had to change clothes every couple of hours because they were so drenched that I could wring the fluid from them.

Except for the very first visit, I always drove to my dad, and this visit was no different. I arrived, and after our greetings, his new wife asked if I'd like to borrow a t-shirt so she could toss mine into her dryer because the material was dark with my perspiration. Mortified, I mumbled something about having had too much coffee and accepted her offer. I decided right then I couldn't back out of bringing the topic up with my dad; there was no way I could continue the way things were or keep living the way I was. I needed to tell him; I needed him to know I was telling the truth back then and I needed to know if he would finally believe me. When his wife went upstairs to check if my shirt was dry yet, I turned to my dad, clearing my throat.

"Dad," I started, but couldn't maintain eye contact, dropping my gaze to stare at a picture on the wall over his right shoulder. "You remember back when we were living in Aunt Sissy's house after Mom left and took everyone else with her?"

"That was a long time ago," he replied, twisting his head from side to side like he was stretching his neck.

I realized I might vomit with my words, but I had to take that risk; I couldn't keep them in anymore. "You remember when I told you that my cousin touched me? You didn't believe me, but I wasn't lying. I was telling you the truth—he molested me."

He tilted his head to one side and inhaled loudly. "You don't remember things right," he said.

My body froze as my eyes flooded with tears, waiting, but that was all he offered. As my heart started again, racing faster than ever, I was screaming at him in my mind, demanding that he explain to me how my cousin touching me between my legs while I cried and begged him to let me go, how my cousin pinning me against him so hard that I couldn't breathe for several seconds, how my cousin rubbing his erection into my backside while he did those things was something I didn't remember right. How my devastation when he told me I was lying and made me promise I'd never tell another soul was not remembering things right.

I'd spent almost my entire life reliving that horrific moment in time, but he'd just told me I wasn't remembering things right. How could he say that?

I said none of those things, though. Instead, I sat, silent, until his wife returned and I thanked her for bringing my shirt. I said very little for the rest of the time I was there that day, everything progressing through topics they normally did. It wasn't until I got into my car and pulled away from the curb in front of his house that everything I *hadn't* said came pouring out of me as I screamed at my windshield, my tears pouring down my face. I was about halfway home when the anger began to subside and I was left with two equally dominating emotions.

The first, I'd expected—a heartbreaking sorrow that my father not only didn't believe me then, but was now effectively attempting to remove that narrative from my life entirely by questioning my memory.

The second emotion, however, was *not* expected. It was something akin to pride. I may not have figured out how to deal with that event in my past, and my dad may not have provided the associated closure I was looking for, but I *knew* what happened, and by bringing it up—regardless of his reaction and response—I'd stuck up for my not-quite-seven-year-old self for the first time in my life and the little girl inside me would be eternally grateful for my courage.

dominoes

The accounting firm I work for recently hosted a panel of speakers for the 2021 International Day for the Elimination of Racial Discrimination. In addition to members of global firm leadership, there was a guest speaker: Emmanuel Acho. If you're unfamiliar with the name, he is a Nigerian-American national football analyst, former NFL player, and vocal advocate for the elimination of racism. He hosts a podcast and recently published a book, both by the name of *Uncomfortable Conversations With A Black Man*. During his portion, he talked about how eliminating discrimination, effecting any meaningful change, doesn't start with trying to change everyone's point of view—it starts with changing that of your neighbors.

He likened his perspective to setting up dominoes. Ultimately, the goal is to knock them all down in rapid succession, one after the other, until every last domino has toppled over. But that very first domino doesn't have to worry about knocking over that last one—it only needs to worry about knocking over the second one. The second one knocks over the third, which knocks over the fourth, and so on. He posited that through tough, meaningful conversations with your neighbors, you can impact their thoughts and behaviors related to discrimination. In turn, they will then impact their neighbors, and over time, many people have been impacted. You didn't have to try to reach everyone.

This concept makes a lot of sense to me. I think about how when I have a great or terrible experience, the first thing I do is tell people about it. "You should try…" or "Stay away from…" If I hear the name of a company that my friend's friend had a fabulous experience with, I'm likely to try them out. Likewise, if that friend's friend had an awful experience, I'm likely to pass and continue looking for another company that suits my needs. It's the concept behind the terms "word of mouth" and "grassroots" and it's real. It's powerful.

As an author, my "neighbors" are my readers, the people—like you—who pick up my book and absorb my words, digest the stories my words are conveying. Even before that, my neighbors are my editors, my proofreaders, my beta readers. My family, my friends.

Throughout my writing career, as I've sent manuscripts and blog posts and article drafts to editors and beta readers, I've received responses that included stories of memories that were surfaced, self-realizations that were life-changing, healing journeys that were kickstarted, because of sharing my past, my pain.

dominoes

As soon as I shared my blog post *Let's Talk About Consent, Baby*, someone commented that they'd learned something. On another post, a different person shared a similar experience from their past. Yet another inspired someone to write their story down. Several have garnered thanks because my words helped the reader realize they weren't alone.

Finding Annie brought in reviews and emails from readers who were touched by the topics addressed, grateful for the way they were realistically portrayed. Readers who felt less alone in the world and had hope they could no longer feel broken and would find peace because of the characters I'd crafted. Men and women who felt seen for the first time, others who expressed gratitude that I'd given them a new perspective and understanding of survivors. Others who were going to share my writing with their loved ones so those loved ones would have a better understanding of them.

When I received my memoir, *resilient*, back from my second editor, I found a number of non-editorial comments from her. Some were expressions of compassion for the experiences in my earlier life, but others weren't. There were places she said she'd harbored anger on my behalf until she'd read my last chapters, that I had inspired her to be compassionate to those whose errors had harmed me as well. Other places she said that my introspection, my self-analysis of my reactive behavior opened up doors for her, provided her with a new understanding of herself and others.

moments of *extraordinary* courage

After my initial draft of the first chapter of this book, "the silencing," I read it to my husband. In part, I simply wanted to read it out loud to help me with any inconsistencies in flow. I also was secretly proud of what I'd written on my first pass, something that occurs infrequently enough that it engenders excitement when it does. My husband tends to be a silent listener unless he finds something hilariously funny, taking everything in, processing, and speaking and reacting after. But during this reading, he snorted during my first paragraph—the same sound I'd made the first time I read the quote included there. He murmured quietly to himself a number of times and had a few sharp intakes of breath. And when I was finished, he started talking immediately.

He told me about moments of silencing in his own life that my words had inspired to loosen and bring to the surface for him. He emotionally described the way he'd felt and why, explained that hearing me write about it the way I had for some reason allowed him to feel and accept how painful those moments had been rather than keeping them locked away.

My editor messaged me while this book was with her after it was drafted. She told me she'd been working on her editorial pass and had to stop, that my chapter "#metoo" had inspired her to write her own #MeToo story down for the first time, that reading about my moment of courage had inspired one in her. That since she'd met me and read my writing, she'd realized she had a right to have a voice, was allowed to speak and tell her story. My bravery had encouraged hers.

I've always wanted to do my part to make this world a better place. I've never been content with sitting on the sidelines while injustice raged around me, never been comfortable with staying quiet when someone else was being wronged. I've thirsted for justice in the world, for fairness and equality and compassion and love since I was very young. I've wanted to eradicate anything that could lead to the types of experiences I've had in order to spare others from that anguish. Having children only tossed gasoline on that fire inside me, made that desire burn brighter and hotter; I have to do everything I can to make the world a better place for my children. For all children.

Having children has also taught me something else. I can crusade for others until my dying breath and my daughters will learn that we stick up for those who can't do so for themselves. I can support the causes I believe in, no matter the cost, and my daughters will learn the integrity of always doing the right thing. I can forgive and show kindness to others and my daughters will learn to be compassionate. But my daughters will never learn to do those things for themselves—they will never learn *self*-compassion or *self*-forgiveness or *self*-worth if I don't first demonstrate by doing those things for myself.

Likewise, I can tell someone a thousand times that I understand them, but they won't truly feel understood until they know I have shared experience.

Telling someone they aren't alone isn't the same as *showing* them they aren't alone, and it's the impact of showing that's needed to topple that first domino. So, I've shown you some of my most difficult moments of courage within these pages and sent my domino tumbling toward you, my dear reader. My neighbor.

The next domino is up to you.

"Loving ourselves through the process of owning our story is the bravest thing we will ever do."

-Brené Brown

acknowledgements

There are always so many people who are part of a book coming to life and ending up in someone else's hands, so many people who contributed in one way or another. Writing this section to thank them is one of the hardest parts of writing the whole book—at least for me. I'm afraid I'll forget someone until it's too late or that I won't adequately express their pivotal role or my gratitude. And that challenge is compounded when I'm writing nonfiction because there are so many people who were part of my life and in that unique way contributed to what you're holding as the reader.

I'll start this time by thanking the people in my life who contributed in a pivotal and positive way to me becoming the person I am, the person who is now able to share those most intimate and difficult parts of my life in order to help others. Mom, when I was growing up in foster care because you were unable to raise my siblings and me, I never thought I'd thank you for anything. Despite everything else that happened, though, you did something remarkable—you believed me when I most desperately needed you to. Without that experience, I never would have trusted again.

Likewise, I want to thank my foster mom, the woman who raised me from the time I was eight; you not only gave me a life and opportunities I never would otherwise have, you also taught me to have the courage to never give up when I believed in something, and that it's never too late for self-examination or to do the right thing. I would not be the woman I am if it weren't for you.

Thank you to my husband, my sister, my friends—you've all supported me in various ways, directly and indirectly, as I've embarked on this journey of transformation, courage, and authenticity. You've all remained by my side, steadfastly cheering me on, as I've transformed into someone who is, in many ways, unrecognizable from the person you knew before. I wouldn't still be on this path today without you all in my life.

I am deeply grateful for the unexpected relationships I've formed during my journey, especially Melissa and Rebekah, who have been a safe place for me emotionally at different times over the last few years, and who were pillars of support when I was overtaken by fear—there are moments of courage within these pages that never would have happened without you and I am deeply, eternally grateful. An extra thank you and a hug here to Melissa for always having my back, for always being up for reading anything I send, and for playing an unexpected and vital role in my healing journey. I can't express what that has meant to me.

acknowledgements

Jenn, thank you for being such a wonderful manager and friend, for caring about me as a person and for your support of my healing and my writing; this wouldn't be happening without you.

Deep thanks are also due to everyone who participated in getting this book to production—my editors, Olivia and Kayli, who always make time for me even when it's less than convenient and understand me in ways others don't; my cover designer, Emily, who took a risk on a new client with very little notice; my e-book formatter, Jo, for taking on this project with a quick turnaround; advanced readers and reviewers; and every single person I pestered (relentlessly) for an opinion so many times they couldn't even tell that something had changed because I'm a perfectionist.

A special thanks to those who stepped out of the silence before me, especially Brené Brown, Kathy Parker, Rachael Brooks, and Chanel Miller; you're inspiring courage not only in me, but all those around you.

Sometimes the last in a list is a statement about relative importance. Other times it's because it was the most difficult for some reason or other. In this case, it's definitely the latter. Even though I'm a writer, I sometimes find it exceedingly difficult to articulate my thoughts and feelings, and those are the things I put off as I try to untangle the emotions involved so I can begin to assign language to them in a coherent manner. Frankly, I don't want to even thank this person because "thank you" feels so... trite and plain old *inadequate*. Instead, I offer this acknowledgement. Olivia, my editor and my friend, none of this would be happening without you; without your moments of quiet support and cacophonous outrage, your steady belief in me and what I'm doing in this world, your ability to hear the things I can't yet say and understand the feelings I can't yet name and see the goals I can't yet explain, your uncanny knack for knowing what I need to hear and when to restore my sometimes shaky confidence and elusive courage. Not just my writing, but—more importantly—my life, is, and forever will be, better because of you.

further reading

Blog Posts and Essays by Katherine Turner

Let's Talk About Consent, Baby
(https://kturnerwrites.com/2019/09/20/lets-talk-about-consent-baby/)

The Art of Waterproofing
(https://kturnerwrites.com/2020/03/06/the-art-of-waterproofing/)

Why I Write What I Write
(https://kturnerwrites.com/2019/08/30/my-story/)

Losing Face
(https://kturnerwrites.com/2020/06/12/losing-face/)

Mixed in America: A Perspective on Discrimination
(https://kturnerwrites.com/2020/08/07/mixed-in-america/)

We are the Storm
(https://kturnerwrites.com/2020/12/18/we-are-the-storm/)

Un-Silent
(https://www.forwomenwhoroar.com/nonfiction/2020/11/5/un-silent)

Books

resilient by Katherine Turner
Know My Name by Chanel Miller
Beads: A Memoir about Falling Apart and Putting Yourself Back Together Again by Rachael Brooks
The Unravelled Heart by Kathy Parker
Train Gone by Rebekah Mallory
all about love by bell hooks
Braving the Wilderness by Brené Brown
The Gifts of Imperfection by Brené Brown
I Thought It Was Just Me (but it isn't) by Brené Brown

Websites

Katherine Turner
(www.kturnerwrites.com)
Don't Ask Liv
(www.dontaskliv.wordpress.com)
This Girl Unravelled
(https://kathyparker.com.au/)
Rachael Brooks
(www.rachaelbrooks.com)
Rebekah Mallory
(www.rebekahmallory.com)
Brené Brown
(http://www.brenebrown.com/)
Uncomfortable Conversations With a Black Man
(https://uncomfortableconvos.com/)

about the author

Katherine Turner is an award-winning author, editor, and a life-long reader and writer. She grew up in foster care from the age of eight and is passionate about improving the world through literature, empathy, and understanding. In addition to writing books, Katherine blogs about mental health, trauma, and the need for compassion on her website www.kturnerwrites.com. She lives in northern Virginia with her husband and two children.

by katherine turner

Fiction

<u>Life Imperfect Series</u>

Finding Annie

Willow Wishes

Non-Fiction

moments of extraordinary courage

resilient: a memoir

www.ingramcontent.com/pod-product-compliance
Lightning Source LLC
Chambersburg PA
CBHW021108080526
44587CB00010B/431